D0707855

THE GREATEST
ROCK & POP
MISCELLANY EVER!

Printed and bound in Great Britain by MPG Books Ltd, Bodmin

Published exclusively for Ottakar's PLC by Sanctuary Publishing Limited,
Sanctuary House, 45–53 Sinclair Road, London W14 0NS, United Kingdom

ISBN: 1-84567-135-X

THE GREATEST
ROCK & POP
MISCELLANY EVER!

OTTAKAR'S

FROM ARNOLD TO ENGELBERT
— SINGERS' REAL NAMES —

Adam Ant – Stuart Goddard
Alice Cooper – Vincent Furnier
Billie Holiday – Eleanora Fagan
Billy Idol – William Board
Billy Ocean – Leslie Sebastian Charles
Bob Dylan – Robert Zimmerman
Bono – Paul Hewson
Boy George – George O'Dowd
Buddy Holly – Charles Hardin Holley
Cher – Cherilyn Sarkisian
Cliff Richard – Harry Webb
Courtney Love – Love Michelle Harrison
David Bowie – David Jones
E (Eels) – Mark Oliver Everett
Elton John – Reginald Dwight
Elvis Costello – Declan McManus
Engelbert Humperdinck – Arnold Dorsey
Eric Clapton – Eric Clapp
Gary Glitter – Paul Gadd
George Michael – Georgios Panayiotou
Huey Lewis – Hugh Cregg

— STARS BEHIND BARS —
PART ONE

Sid Vicious – As a prime suspect in girlfriend Nancy Spungen's death, Vicious spent two weeks in New York prisons before committing suicide.

Bobby Brown – The R&B star – these days best known for his marriage to Whitney Houston – has spent more time in jail than in the studio, usually for drug offences.

Gary Glitter – The glam-rock star spent four months in prison in late 1999 after computer repairers found child pornography on his computer, and left the country soon afterwards.

Ian Brown – After a 1998 argument on a plane – Brown says he was framed, the judge thought otherwise – the Stone Roses frontman was convicted of threatening behaviour and spent two months in prison.

— EVEN BETTER THAN THE REAL THING —

23 tribute bands from around the world:

2U (U2)
Abbalanche (ABBA)
Abbey Rode (The Beatles)
AC-DShe (AC/DC)
Alike Cooper (Alice Cooper)
Back Stabbath (Black Sabbath)
By Jovi (Bon Jovi)
Fab Faux (The Beatles)
Fake No More (Faith No More)
Four Fighters (Foo Fighters)
Led Zepagain (Led Zeppelin)
Mandonna (Madonna)
Once More Into The Bleach (Blondie)
Phil Haley and His Comments (Bill Haley & The Comets)
Sack Blabbath (Black Sabbath)
Sample Minds (Simple Minds)
Sisters of Murphy (Sisters of Mercy)
Stereophonies (Stereophonics)
Stung (Sting)
Textas (Texas)
The Rolling Clones (The Rolling Stones)
Tin Lizzy (Thin Lizzy)
Who's Who (The Who)

— ONLY IN NORWAY... —

Sheepish behaviour: In 2003, Norwegian group Mayhem fractured a fan's skull with a severed sheep's head when it slipped from lead singer Maniac's knife. Mayhem, maniac, on-stage butchery... you just know they're a death metal band.

Sex on stage: In 2004, Tommy Hol Ellingsen and his girlfriend Leona Johannsson were arrested after having sex on stage at a Norwegian rock concert. They were doing it 'to save the environment'. Those crazy Norwegians!

— ACTING UP —

Keanu Reeves: Played bass in grunge band Dogstar, whose two albums were derided by almost everybody.

Bruce Willis: Spent most of the '80s and '90s murdering soul classics which, amazingly, sold millions.

Russell Crowe: Singer in lumpen rockers 30-odd Foot of Grunts. Unlikely to be the next U2.

Johnny Depp: Played guitar with Noel Gallagher and on Shane McGowan's 'That Woman's Got Me Drinking'.

Juliette Lewis: The Natural Born Killer launched her musical career in mid-2004 in a blaze of publicity, but hadn't released any records as we went to press, although she features on The Prodigy's new album *Always Outnumbered, Never Outgunned*.

William Shatner: Shatner's pretentious spoken word versions of songs such as 'Lucy In The Sky With Diamonds' have gained a cult following among the 'so bad it's good' crowd. Shatner is currently working on a new crop of cover versions, including Pulp's 'Common People'.

Kevin Bacon: Sings in The Bacon Brothers with brother Michael. Released their fourth album in 2004.

David Hasselhoff: Has released seven solo albums since the mid-'80s. A huge pop star in Germany.

Martine McCutcheon: Reached number 1 in 1999 with 'Perfect Moment', and enjoyed a brief run as Eliza Doolittle in the West End production of *My Fair Lady*, but sensibly decided to return to the day job.

Billy Bob Thornton: One of the few actor-cum-musicians to get good reviews from the serious music press, Thornton's solo efforts have attracted a small but enthusiastic following.

— FASCINATING FACS —

A selection from the first 100 items in legendary label Factory Records'
iconic catalogue:

FAC1	Concert poster
FAC2	*A Factory Sampler*: twin 7" single featuring Joy Division and others
FAC3,4	Concert posters
FAC5	A Certain Ratio's 'All Night Party' single
FAC6	OMD's 'Electricity' single
FAC7	Paper and envelopes
FAC8	Egg timer
FAC9	*The Factory Flick*: footage of Joy Division, A Certain Ratio
FACT10	Joy Division: *Unknown Pleasures*
FAC12	Distractions: 'Time Goes By So Slow' single
FAC13	Joy Division: 'Transmission' single
FACT14	Durutti Column: *The Return Of The Durutti Column* LP
FACT16C	A Certain Ratio: *The Graveyard And The Ballroom* cassette
FAC18	Section 25: 'Girls Don't Count' single
FAC19	John Downe: 'It's Hard To Be An Egg' single
FAC20	A Certain Ratio film (never made)
FAC21	Badge
FAC22	A Certain Ratio: 'Flight' 12"
FAC23	Joy Division: 'Love Will Tear Us Apart' single
FACT24	*A Factory Quartet* double LP
FACT25	Joy Division: *Closer*
FAC28	Joy Division: 'Komakino' single
FACT30	Sex Pistols: 'The Heyday' (documentary on cassette)
FAC31	Minny Pops: 'Dolphin Spurt' single
FAC32	Crispy Ambulance: 'Unsightly & Serene' single
FAC33	New Order: 'Ceremony' single
FAC34	ESG: 'You're No Good' single
FACT35	A Certain Radio: *To Each...* LP
FAC36	USA advert for Joy Division's *Closer*
FACT37	Joy Division: 'Here Are The Young Men' video
FACT38	A Certain Ratio: 'Below The Canal' video (never finished)
FACT40	Joy Division: *Still* LP
FACT42	A Certain Ratio: 'The Double' 12"
FAC43	Royal Family & The Poor: 'Art Dream Dominion' single
FACT44	Durutti Column: *LC* LP

FACT46	The Video Circus (preview video)
FAC47	Factory logo
FAC48	Kevin Hewick: 'Ophelia's Drinking Song' single
FAC49	Swamp Children: 'Little Voices' 12"
FACT50	New Order: *Movement* LP
FAC51	The Hacienda nightclub
FAC51B	New Order: 'Merry Xmas From The Hacienda' flexi-disc
FAC52	A Certain Ratio: 'Waterline' 12"
FAC53	New Order: 'Everything's Gone Green' single
FAC54	Video of the Hacienda being constructed
FACT55	A Certain Ratio: *Sextet* LP
FACT56	A Factory Video
FAC57	Minny Pops: 'Secret Story' single
FAC59	52nd Street: 'Look Into My Eyes' single
FAC61	Lawsuit against Factory by producer Martin Hannett
FAC63	New Order: 'Temptation' single
FACT65	A Certain Ratio: *I'd Like To See You Again* LP
FAC68	Section 25: 'Back To Wonder' single
FACT71	A Factory Outing (video)
FAC72	A Certain Ratio: 'I Need Someone Tonight' single
FAC73	New Order: 'Blue Monday' single
FACT74	Durutti Column: *Another Setting* LP
FACT75	New Order: *Power, Corruption And Lies* LP
FACT76	Jazz Defektors: *The Movie* (unreleased)
FACT77	New Order: 'Taras Shevchenko' video
FAC78	James: 'Jimone' single
FACT80	Stockholm Monsters: *Alma Mater* LP
FAC81	Factory 1st International Congress notepaper
FAC82	Cabaret Voltaire: 'Yashar' 12"
FAC83	Flyer for the Hacienda's first birthday party
FAC86	Cardboard Hacienda model kit
FAC88	The Wake: 'Talk About The Past' single
FACT89	John Dowie: 'Dowie' video
FACT90	Section 25: *From The Hip* LP
FAC91	Computer game (never finished)
FAC92	Marcel King: 'Reach For Love' single
FAC93	New Order: 'Confusion' single
FAC97	Streetlife: 'Act On Instinct' single
FAC98	Swing – the Hacienda's hairdressing salon
FAC99	Dental bill for Rob Gretton, New Order's manager
FACT100	New Order: *Low Life* LP

(many, many more FACs at http://listen.to/factory)

— BANNED IN THE USA —

In the wake of 9/11, radio giant Clear Channel sent its stations a list of 150 songs with 'questionable lyrics' that they might want to refrain from playing. The list included the following:

AC/DC – 'Highway to Hell'
The Animals – 'We Gotta Get Out Of This Place'
Arthur Brown – 'Fire'
The Bangles – 'Walk Like An Egyptian'
Beastie Boys – 'Sabotage'
The Beatles – 'Lucy In The Sky With Diamonds'
Billy Joel – 'Only The Good Die Young'
Black Sabbath – 'War Pigs'
Bruce Springsteen – 'Goin' Down'
Carole King – 'I Feel The Earth Move'
Cat Stevens – 'Morning Has Broken'
Dave Matthews Band – 'Crash Into Me'
Edwin Starr/Bruce Springsteen – 'War'
Foo Fighters – 'Learn To Fly'
Jan and Dean – 'Dead Man's Curve'
Led Zeppelin – 'Stairway To Heaven'
Nine Inch Nails – 'Head Like A Hole'
Paul McCartney and Wings – 'Live And Let Die'
Peter, Paul and Mary – 'Leavin' On A Jet Plane'
All Rage Against The Machine songs
Queen – 'Another One Bites The Dust'
Red Hot Chili Peppers – 'Aeroplane'
REM – 'It's The End Of The World As We Know It (And I Feel Fine)'
Simon and Garfunkel – 'Bridge Over Troubled Water'
Surfaris – 'Wipe Out'
U2 – 'Sunday Bloody Sunday'

— CREED CRACK UP —

You know you're in trouble when your own fans take you to court, but that's exactly what happened to US rockers Creed in 2003. Four fans sued the band for a substandard performance, alleging that singer Scott Stapp was too drunk to perform. The band took the unprecedented step of apologising to all their fans for being rubbish, and split up a few months later.

— FRANKIE SAY... —

In the mid-1980s, no self-respecting pop fan was without one of Frankie Goes To Hollywood's iconic 'Frankie say...' T-shirts.

There were three versions, all based on Katharine Hamnett's 'Ban Nuclear Weapons Now' design:

- Frankie Say Relax Don't Do It
- Frankie Say War Hide Yourself
- Frankie Say Arm The Unemployed

Other designs – which started 'Frankie Says' instead of 'Frankie Say' – were fakes.

— BARE-FACED CHEEK —

Nine stars who have showed their bits...

Adam Clayton, U2:	Displays 'little Adam' on the cover of *Achtung Baby*
Jim Morrison, The Doors:	Arrested for indecent exposure at a gig in Miami, 1969
Rage Against The Machine:	Appeared naked on stage to protest against censorship in 1993
John Lennon:	Posed naked with Yoko for the cover of *Two Virgins*
Red Hot Chili Peppers:	Famous used sports socks to preserve their modesty
Nick Oliveri, ex-QOTSA:	Routinely played naked
Kurt Cobain:	Flashed photographers at a gig in 1992
Courtney Love:	Regularly caught on camera in some disarray, both on and off stage
Blink 182:	Appeared naked in the video for 'What's My Age Again?'

— METAL GENRES —

Metal: Short for 'Heavy Metal': pulverisingly loud rock music that rarely looks on the bright side of life.

Black Metal: Ultra-dark heavy metal that has an unhealthy fascination with the occult.

Death Metal: *Drum* Magazine calls Death Metal 'a tangled blur of indecipherable growling, guitar shreds and breakneck beats'. Even less cheery than other forms of metal.

False Metal: As in 'Death to False Metal!'. Any sort of Metal that isn't by your favourite bands.

Nu-Metal: Ultra-commercial synthesis of rock and rap that brought us Limp Bizkit.

NWOBHM: The New Wave of British Heavy Metal. Iron Maiden, Saxon, Def Leppard etc. 'Death to False Metal!' was their catchphrase.

Speed Metal: Insanely fast genre of heavy metal where speed of playing is the most important thing.

— CRIMES AGAINST MUSIC —

The 10 worst songs of all time, as voted by readers of DotMusic:

1. 'The Birdie Song' – The Tweets
2. 'Teletubbies Say Eh-Oh!' – The Teletubbies
3. 'Barbie Girl' – Aqua
4. 'Agadoo' – Black Lace
5. 'I Should Be So Lucky' – Kylie Minogue
6. 'We're Going To Ibiza' – Vengaboys
7. 'Grandma We Love You' – St Winifred's School Choir
8. 'Shaddap You Face' – Joe Dolce
9. 'Achy Breaky Heart' – Billy Ray Cyrus
10. 'The Lady In Red' – Chris De Burgh

— THE WORLD'S MOST DEPRESSING SONG —

Songs are banned for all kinds of reasons – political controversy, obscenity, glamorising things that shouldn't be glamorised – but 'Gloomy Sunday' was banned because it killed people. The song, written in 1933 by composer Rezso Seress, developed a reputation as the 'suicide song', a song so depressing that if you heard it, you might be plunged into a bottomless pit of despair. Reports from Hungary, where 'Gloomy Sunday' originated, suggest that the lyrics were used in countless suicide notes.

Seress's crushingly bleak original went through a number of revisions – it was amended by poet Laszlo Javor, whose version was in turn translated by English lyricists Sam M Lewis and Desmond Carter. Billie Holiday covered the song in 1941, but even though her version added a less pessimistic third verse, the song's reputation persisted and radio stations throughout the world deemed it too dangerous to broadcast.

As the excellent Gloomy Sunday site (www.phespirit.info/gloomysunday) notes: 'Despite all such bans, "Gloomy Sunday" continued to be recorded and sold. People continued to buy the recordings; some committed suicide. Rezso Seress jumped to his death from his flat in 1968.'

— BNTAA —
Band Names That Are Acronyms

ABBA: Agnetha, Bjorn, Benny, Anni-Frid
Carter USM: Carter the Unstoppable Sex Machine
D12: Dirty Dozen
ELO: Electric Light Orchestra
ELP: Emerson, Lake and Palmer
EPMD: Erick and Parrish Making Dollars
KLF: Copyright Liberation Front
KMFDM: Kill Mother F***ing Depeche Mode
LFO: Low Frequency Oscillation
MC5: Motor City Five
N*E*R*D: No one Ever Really Dies
NWA: Niggaz With Attitude
OMD: Orchestral Manoeuvres in the Dark
REM: Rapid Eye Movement
SLF: Stiff Little Fingers
WASP: We Are Sexual Perverts

— BIG HITTERS —

How many search results does Google find for your favourite band?

Britney Spears*	5,820,000
The Beatles	5,510,000
U2	4,560,000
REM	3,830,000
The Who	2,500,000
The Rolling Stones	2,210,000
Aerosmith	1,850,000
Radiohead	1,760,000
Nickelback	1,320,000
Led Zeppelin	932,000
Limp Bizkit	926,000
Franz Ferdinand**	590,000
Fleetwood Mac	477,000
Robson & Jerome	26,000
Fast Food Rockers	17,800
Bonzo Dog Doo-Dah Band	10,700

* The hits for Britney may include some distinctly non-musical sites
** Includes sites about Archduke Franz Ferdinand, whose assassination led to the First World War

— HOW TO HAVE A NUMBER ONE (THE EASY WAY) —

The KLF's legendary *How To Have A Number One The Easy Way* is a must-read, but its advice can be distilled into just 100 words:

'[The song must] have a dance groove that will run all the way through the record and that the current buying generation will find irresistible. Secondly, it must be no longer than three minutes and thirty seconds [or] DJs will start fading early or talking over the end, when the chorus is finally being hammered home – the most important part of any record. Thirdly, it must consist of an intro, a verse, a chorus, second verse, a second chorus, a breakdown section, back into a double length chorus and outro. Fourthly, lyrics. You will need some, but not many.'

— YOU'RE NOT GOING OUT DRESSED LIKE THAT —

In late 2003, retailer Woolworth's carried out a survey to find the worst clothes in the world of rock and pop. The fashion disasters included:

Bucks Fizz's detachable skirts
Badly Drawn Boy's tea-cosy hat
MC Hammer's baggy trousers
Geri Halliwell's Union Jack dress
Christina Aguilera's leather chaps
Cher's see-through dress
The Cheeky Girls' gold hotpants
Kate Bush's multi-coloured legwarmers
The Village People's outfits
Meat Loaf's frilly white shirt and 'matching hanky'

— LONG LIVE THE KING! —

According to some, Elvis didn't die: sick of the pressures of fame, he faked his own death so he could return to a normal life. The Elvis Sighting Bulletin Board (www.elvissightingbulletinboard.com) keeps track of his movements; here are some of the most recent entries:

At the Brandenburg Gate, Berlin, with Priscilla
At the Dollywood theme park
In Cook County Prison, Illinois
Working at Betty's Hair Hut, Rock Springs, Wyoming
Eating a whaleburger, Northern Canada
Working as a biology teacher in Lancaster, Lancashire
Fishing naked off Clacton Pier
Buying toilet plungers in a branch of Home Depot, California
Arrested for being drunk in public, Walker County, Texas
Buying frozen peas and fish fingers at the Piggly Wiggly Grocery Store,
Fort Arthur, Texas
Living quietly in Little Rock, Arkansas
Driving badly in Cincinnati, Ohio
Fighting off muggers Batman-style in Salem, Oregon
Living under a bridge in Nottingham
Buying onions in a Norwegian supermarket
Driving a builder's van in Ipswich

— TAT'S ENTERTAINMENT: TATTOOS OF THE STARS — PART ONE

Billie Jo Armstrong (Green Day)

Right arm: circled number 27, two angels: 'Adrienne', 'Joseph', a rose, a small cross, a vine, 'pinhead', a baby smoking a cigar, a tiny black heart; Left arm: 'Jacob', a baby, a clown bracelet, a flower, 'P.U.N.X.'; Hip: 'punks'

Brody Armstrong (Distillers)

Large oriental dragon on right arm, small heart on left wrist, skull and crossbones on left shoulder

Travis Barker (Blink 182)

Chequered design on both sides of neck (race car flag?), 'Can I Say' across collar bones, nude women outlines on opposite sides of upper chest, two different designs above nude women, design between nude women, radio on stomach, large design on mid-lower back, both arms sleeved (one arm contains a Virgin Mary dedicated to his mother), left leg has logo from a Descendents' album

Chester Bennington (Linkin Park)

Koi fish, blue red flames on both wrists, soldier with wings, LINKIN PARK in Old English on lower back, right pinkie finger has gold ring and birthstone, ring finger has same tattoo as his wife, a purple dragon on his right calf

Beyonce

Praying angel on upper left thigh

David Bowie

Lizard on ankle

— UK'S BEST-SELLING CHARITY SINGLES —

Artist	Song	Sales	Year
Elton John	'Candle In The Wind '97'	4.86 million	1997
Band Aid	'Do They Know It's Christmas?'	3.55 million	1984
Various	'Perfect Day'	1.55 million	1997

Source: www.everyhit.com

— ITUNES – BUY TUNES —

Digital downloads sold by the iTunes Music Store

First week sales (USA):	1,000,000
First week sales (Europe):	800,000
First week sales (UK):	450,000
First year sales (USA):	70,000,000

— MAGGIE'S FARM —

30 songs that mention animals in the title

'Ant Music' – Adam And The Ants
'Atomic Dog' – George Clinton
'Black Dog' – Led Zeppelin
'Boris The Spider' – The Who
'Buffalo Soldier' – Bob Marley
'Cool For Cats' – Squeeze
'Crazy Horses' – The Osmonds
'Crocodile Rock' – Elton John
'Doggy Dogg World' – Snoop Doggy Dogg
'Eye Of The Tiger' – Survivor
'Hey Bulldog' – The Beatles
'Hound Dog' – Elvis
'Hungry Like The Wolf' – Duran Duran
'Kiss That Frog' – Peter Gabriel
'Little Red Rooster' – The Rolling Stones
'Peace Frog' – The Doors
'Piggies' – The Beatles
'Rat In Mi Kitchen' – UB40
'Rat Trap' – Boomtown Rats
'Rockin' Robin' – Michael Jackson
'Rocky Racoon' – The Beatles
'The Lion Sleeps Tonight' – Tight Fit
'Tiger Feet' – Mud
'Union Of The Snake' – Duran Duran
'War Pigs' – Black Sabbath
'What's New Pussycat?' – Tom Jones
'When Doves Cry' – Prince
'Who Let The Dogs Out?' – Baha Men
'Who's Gonna Ride Your Wild Horses' – U2
'Wild Horses' – The Rolling Stones

— THE REVOLUTION WILL NOT BE TELEVISED —

Many artists have been banned from MTV – in its early days, an alleged ban on videos by black artists led to Herbie Hancock's video for 'Rockit' featuring disembodied legs so that the video would be broadcast – but some artists go out of their way to court controversy. Madonna has been a particular controversy magnet: her videos for 'Justify My Love' and 'Erotica' were banned, while her 2004 'What It Feels Like For A Girl' was banned due to its excessively violent rampage.

Of course, Madonna isn't the only artist whose videos haven't been aired on MTV. In 2003, the Foo Fighters' video for 'Low' was blacklisted (it featured singer Dave Grohl and actor Jack Black in drag), and System Of A Down's track 'Boom' was blocked as the advertising sales department didn't want to upset the US Army. Even anodyne singer-songwriter Vanessa Carlton has fallen foul of the censors: the video for 'Pretty Baby' had to be recut as it broke MTV's strict 'no bondage' rule.

Some videos are banned because of bad timing – after Janet Jackson bared a breast at the 2004 Superbowl, videos by artists such as Britney Spears were pulled from the schedules for being too 'raunchy'; war-related tracks were dropped during the first and second Gulf wars – but many such bans are deliberate attempts to sell more records: Duran Duran made an unbroadcastable video for their 1981 hit 'Girls On Film', while in the late 1990s bands such as The Prodigy created a number of censor-baiting clips that generated invaluable publicity.

The battle between artists and censors will no doubt continue, but it won't happen on MTV: these days the music channel barely plays videos at all, preferring to fill its schedules with reality shows such as *The Osbournes*, documentaries about rap stars' houses and Jackass-style pranksters.

— OLDEST AND YOUNGEST UK CHART-TOPPERS —

Youngest chart-topper: Jimmy Osmond (aged 9), 1972
Youngest Top 40 act: Microbe (aged 3), 1961
Oldest chart-topper: Louis Armstrong (aged 66 and 10 months), 1968
Oldest Top 40 act: John Lee Hooker (aged 75 and 9 months), 1993

Source: everyhit.com

— A LOAD OF BALLS —

Football may be a beautiful game, but as this crop of World Cup anthems shows, it's rarely resulted in beautiful music.

Year	Song	Artists
1970	'Back Home'	England World Cup Squad
1974	'Here We Are'	England World Cup Squad and Magnum Brass
1982	'This Time (We'll Get It Right)'	England World Cup Squad
1986	'We've Got The Whole World At Our Feet'	England World Cup Squad
1990	'World In Motion'	Englandneworder
1998	'How Does It Feel'	England featuring The Spice Girls and The Lightning Seeds
2002	'We're On The Ball'	Ant & Dec featuring the England Supporters Brass Band

— KILLER KARAOKE —

Ten songs routinely murdered at karaoke clubs:
'American Pie' – Don MacLean
'Angels' – Robbie Williams
'Crazy' – Patsy Cline
'Delilah' – Tom Jones
'I Got You Babe' – Sonny & Cher
'La Bamba' – Richie Valens
'My Way' – Frank Sinatra
'Paradise By The Dashboard Light' – Meatloaf
'Summer Nights' – John Travolta and Olivia Newton John
'Sweet Caroline' – Neil Diamond

— ELVIS'S DRUGS —

When Elvis died in 1977, there were 14 different drugs in his bloodstream. According to the autopsy performed on The King, he overdosed on 'significant amounts' of codeine, methaqualone, ethinamate and various barbiturates; the coroner also found traces of morphine, valium, demerol, meperidine, placidly and chloropheniramine.

— BRITS BEHAVING BADLY—

The Brit Awards is the UK record industry's annual exercise in mutual backslapping. Unfortunately, as the Brits organisers have discovered, pop stars aren't always on their best behaviour...

Samantha Fox and Mick Fleetwood (1989)

The Brit Awards were always broadcast live – until 1989's guest presenters made a memorable mess of, well, everything. Lines were fluffed, guests arrived late and introductions were often wrong: for example, Fox and Fleetwood introduced The Four Tops, only for a bemused Boy George to wander on stage.

The KLF (1992)

After playing a thrash metal version of their dance-pop hit '3AM Eternal', the KLF proceeded to machine-gun the audience (using blank bullets) before announcing that they had left the music industry. The band then delivered a freshly slaughtered sheep to the post-awards party with a note saying 'I Died For You'.

Jarvis Cocker, Pulp (1996)

Irritated by Michael Jackson's messianic performance of 'Earth Song', the Pulp frontman invaded the stage, flicked v-signs and wiggled his backside at the cameras. Police were called and bizarrely, Cocker found himself being defended by comedian and former lawyer Bob Mortimer.

Liam Gallagher (1996)

The Oasis singer isn't renowned for his love of his fellow man, and the 1996 Brits were no exception. On receiving an award from INXS singer Michael Hutchence, he informed the Australian that 'has-beens shouldn't give prizes to gonna-bes'.

Chumbawamba (1998)

Politicians can often be spotted at the Brits, and in 1998 Deputy Prime Minister John Prescott was particularly easy to spot after Chumbawamba singer Danbert Nobacon doused him with a bucket of water.

Brandon Block (2000)

The obscure club DJ invaded the stage as Rolling Stone Ronnie Wood presented the best soundtrack award. The BBC reports: 'The rock veteran ended up throwing a drink over Block, and the two swore at each other as security guards pulled the DJ off'.

— 501-DERS —

Levi's iconic ad campaign for its 501 jeans gave unknown acts a big break and resurrected the careers of some of the world's greatest singers. By the time the campaign ended in 1998, the ads had covered everything from blues and country to modern rock, reggae and electronica:

Louis Armstrong – 'What A Wonderful World'
Babylon Zoo – 'Spaceman'
Bad Company – 'Can't Get Enough Of Your Love'
Johnny Cash – 'Ring Of Fire'
The Clash – 'Should I Stay Or Should I Go'
Eddie Cochran – 'C'mon Everybody'
Cockney Rejects – 'I'm Not A Fool'
Sam Cooke – 'Wonderful World'
Erma Franklin – 'Piece Of My Heart'
Freak Power – 'Turn On, Tune In, Cop Out'
Marvin Gaye – 'I Heard It Through The Grapevine'
Johnny Harris – 'Stepping Stones'
Ben E King – 'Stand By Me'
BB King – 'Ain't Nobody Home'
Steve Miller Band – 'The Joker'
1 Biosphere – 'Novelty Waves'
The Ronettes – 'Be My Baby'
Screamin' Jay Hawkins – 'Heart Attack And Vine'
Shaggy – 'Mr Boombastic'
Percy Sledge – 'When A Man Loves A Woman'
Smoke City – 'Underwater Love'
Stiltskin – 'Inside'
T Rex – '20th Century Boy'
Dinah Washington – 'Mad About The Boy'
Muddy Waters – 'Mannish Boy'

— THE WIT AND WISDOM OF THE GALLAGHERS — PART ONE

'I still love George Harrison as a songwriter in The Beatles, but as a person I think he's a f***ing nipple. And if I ever meet him I'll f***ing tell him. And if you're watching, NIPPLE!'
Liam, *MTV Europe*

'She looks like some f***ing tart from f***ing Newcastle.'
Noel on Christina Aguilera, *Sunday Telegraph*

— WOODSTOCK: THEN AND NOW —

Where the original Woodstock was about peace and love, its 1999 successor was marred by violence, assaults and accusations of corporate exploitation. The line-up was slightly different, too...

THE 1969 LINE-UP

DAY ONE:
Richie Havens	Country Joe McDonald
John B Sebastian	Incredible String Band
Sweetwater	Bert Sommer
Tim Hardin	Ravi Shankar
Melanie	Arlo Guthrie
Joan Baez	

DAY TWO:
Quill	Santana
Canned Heat	Mountain
Janis Joplin	Sly & The Family Stone
Grateful Dead	Creedence Clearwater Revival
The Who	

DAY THREE:
Jefferson Airplane	Joe Cocker
Country Joe & The Fish	Ten Years After
The Band	Blood, Sweat And Tears
Johnny Winter	Crosby, Stills, Nash & Young

DAY FOUR:
Paul Butterfield Blues Band	Sha-Na-Na
Jimi Hendrix	

Source: www.digitaldreamdoor.com

THE 1999 LINE-UP

DAY ONE:
James Brown	G Love and Special Sauce
Jamiroquai	Live
Sheryl Crow	DMX
The Offspring	Korn
Bush	

DAY TWO:

The Tragically Hip

Wyclef Jean

Dave Matthews Band

Limp Bizkit

Metallica

Kid Rock

Counting Crows

Alanis Morissette

Rage Against The Machine

DAY THREE:

Willie Nelson

Everlast

Jewel

Red Hot Chili Peppers

Brian Setzer Orchestra

Elvis Costello

Creed

Source: www.festivalhype.com

— ELVIS'S FRIED PEANUT BUTTER SANDWICH —

One of Elvis's favourite foods was the humble – and highly calorific – fried peanut butter sandwich. To make it you'll need two slices of white bread, two tablespoons of peanut butter, half a banana and two tablespoons of butter.

• Mash the banana with a fork

• Then coat the bread with the banana and peanut butter

• Melt the butter in a frying pan or skillet

• Then fry the sandwich until it's brown on both sides

— IN THE ARMY NOW —

Ten musicians who have served in the armed forces:

Bill Wyman – National Service (UK)

Billy Bragg – UK Army

Elvis – US Army

Ian Astbury – UK Army

Ice T – US Army

Jimi Hendrix – US Army

John Mayall – National Service (UK)

MC Hammer – US Marines

Shaggy – US Marines

Terence Trent D'Arby – US Army

MURDER INC
— (12 MURDERED MUSICIANS) —

Al Jackson (Booker T And The MGs)	Shot in his own home
Bobby Fuller	Found dead and covered with petrol, allegedly at the hands of mobsters
Carlton Barrett (The Wailers)	Shot by gunmen at his home
Don Myrick (Earth, Wind & Fire)	Shot by police
Felix Pappalardi (Mountain)	Killed by his wife
Jaco Pastorius (Weather Report)	Killed by a nightclub bouncer
John Lennon	Shot in New York by Mark Chapman
Marvin Gaye	Shot by his father
Notorious BIG	Shot outside a party
Peter Tosh	Killed by burglars
Sam Cooke	Shot in a motel after an altercation with a woman
Tupac Shakur	Shot outside a nightclub, possibly in revenge for the death of Notorious BIG

— THOSE CRAZY GERMANS —

German techno-metallers Rammstein's stage show is notorious: in a typical evening each member of the band will have set themselves on fire, and the band's singer will simulate sex with the keyboard player before 'orgasming' over the crowd. At the end of the show, the drummer leaves by piloting a rubber raft over the audience's heads. Who says Germans don't have a sense of humour?

— THE YEAR IN SONG —

'Spring Haze' – Tori Amos
'Cruel Summer' – Bananarama
'Forever Autumn' – The Moody Blues
'Hazy Shade Of Winter' – Simon and Garfunkel

Or:
'Four Seasons In One Day' – Crowded House

— THE STRANGE STORY OF 'STRANGE FRUIT' —

'Strange Fruit' is one of the most controversial – and powerful – songs of all time, and it's one of the few songs that genuinely changed the world.

The song started life as a poem by schoolteacher Abel Meeropol, who was disturbed by a photograph that depicted the lynching of a black man in America's deep south. He adopted the pen name Lewis Allan and wrote the poem ('Southern trees bear a strange fruit, blood on the leaves and blood at the root') in the late 1930s.

The poem caught the attention of a nightclub manager, who passed it on to 24-year-old singer Billie Holiday; however, while Holiday wanted to record the song, her record company refused. She went to another label and released the song in 1939, and it was quickly adopted by the anti-lynching movement.

While the song became an anthem for civil rights, it wasn't universally popular. Holiday was often abused – sometimes physically – by outraged nightclub patrons when she performed the song, radio stations wouldn't play it, and *Time* Magazine described the song as 'a prime piece of musical propaganda'. Nevertheless activists sent copies of the record to US congressmen, and the song became a rallying cry against racism. As Samuel Grafton wrote in the *New York Post* in 1939, 'Even now, as I think of it, the short hair on the back of my neck tightens and I want to hit someone... If the anger of the exploited ever mounts high enough in the South, it now has its Marseillaise.' Or as Michael Meeropol, Abel's adopted son, told America's *PBS* channel: 'Until the last racist is dead, 'Strange Fruit' is relevant.

— 10 STRANGE MUSICAL COLLABORATIONS —

Aerosmith/Run DMC – 'Walk This Way'
Anthrax/Public Enemy – 'Bring The Noise'
KLF/Tammy Wynette – 'Justified And Ancient'
Nick Cave/Kylie Minogue – 'Where The Wild Roses Grow'
Bono/Frank Sinatra – 'I've Got You Under My Skin'
Art Of Noise/Tom Jones – 'Kiss'
Pet Shop Boys/Dusty Springfield – 'What Have I Done To Deserve This?'
Willie Nelson/Julio Iglesias – 'To All The Girls I've Loved Before'
The Fat Boys/The Beach Boys– 'Wipe Out'
U2/Pavarotti– 'Miss Sarajevo'

— EUROVISION WINNERS —

The Eurovision Song Contest is an annual battle between supposedly peaceful countries, where old rivalries dictate voting patterns and Norway famously gets 'nil points'. The list of winners is a catalogue of the great, the good and the utterly terrifying since the 1950s.

Year	Song	Artist	Country
2004	'Wild Dance'	Ruslana	Ukraine
2003	'Everyway That I Can'	Sertab Erener	Turkey
2002	'I Wanna'	Marie N	Latvia
2001	'Everybody'	Tanel Padar, Dave Benton & 2XL	Estonia
2000	'Fly On The Wings Of Love'	Olsen Brothers	Denmark
1999	'Take Me To Your Heaven'	Charlotte Nilsson	Sweden
1998	'Diva'	Dana International	Israel
1997	'Love Shine A Light'	Katrina and the Waves	UK
1996	'The Voice'	Eimear Quinn	Ireland
1995	'Nocturne'	Secret Garden	Norway
1994	'Rock 'n' Roll Kids'	Paul Harrington & Charlie McGettigan	Ireland
1993	'In Your Eyes'	Niamh Kavanagh	Ireland
1992	'Why Me?'	Linda Martin	Ireland
1991	'Fångad Av En Stormvind'	Carola	Sweden
1990	'Insieme:1992'	Toto Cutugno	Italy
1989	'Rock Me'	Riva	Yugoslavia
1988	'Ne Partez Pas Sans Moi'	Celine Dion	Switzerland
1987	'Hold Me Now'	Johnny Logan	Ireland
1986	'J'Aime La Vie'	Sandra Kim	Belgium
1985	'La Det Swing'e	Bobbysocks	Norway
1984	'Diggi Loo-Diggi Ley'	Herreys	Sweden
1983	'Si La Vie Est Cadeau'	Corinne Hermes	Luxembourg
1982	'Ein Bisschen Frieden'	Nicole	Germany
1981	'Making Your Mind Up'	Bucks Fizz	UK
1980	'What's Another Year'	Johnny Logan	Ireland
1979	'Hallelujah'	Milk & Honey	Israel
1978	'A Ba Ni Bi'	Yizhar Cohen & Alphabeta	Israel
1977	'L'Oiseau Et L'Enfant'	Marie Myriam	France
1976	'Save Your Kisses For Me'	Brotherhood of Man	UK

1975	'Ding Dinge Dong'	Teach-in	Netherlands
1974	'Waterloo'	ABBA	Sweden
1973	'Tu Te Reconnaitras'	Anne-Marie David	Luxembourg
1972	'Apres Toi'	Vicky Leandros	Luxembourg
1971	'Un Banc, Un Arbre, Une Rue'	Severine	Monaco
1970	'All Kinds Of Everything'	Dana	Ireland
1969*	'Vivo Cantando'	Salome	Spain
	'Boom Bang-A-Bang'	Lulu	UK
	'De Troubadour'	Lennie Kuhr	Netherlands
	'Un Jour, Un Enfant'	Frida Boccara	France
1968	'La La La'	Massiel	Spain
1967	'Puppet On A String'	Sandie Shaw	UK
1966	'Merci Cherie'	Udo Jurgens	Austria
1965	'Poupee De Cire, Poupee De Son'	France Gall	Luxembourg
1964	'No Ho L'Eta'	Gigliola Cinquetti	Italy
1963	'Dansevise'	Grethe & Jorgen Ingmann	Denmark
1962	'Un Premier Amour'	Isabelle Aubret	France
1961	'Nous Les Amoureux'	Jean-Claude Pascal	Luxembourg
1960	'Tom Pillibi'	Jacqueline Boyer	France
1959	'Een Beetje'	Teddy Scholten	Netherlands
1958	'Dors Mon Amour'	Andre Claveau	France
1957	'Net Als Toen'	Corry Brokken	Netherlands
1956	'Refrain'	Lys Assia	Switzerland

* In 1969 four countries tied for first place with 18 points each.

— WHISTLE WHILE YOU WORK —

10 classic tunes featuring whistling:

'Always Look On The Bright Side Of Life' – Monty Python
'Don't Worry Be Happy' – Bobby McFerrin
'Games Without Frontiers' – Peter Gabriel
'Jealous Guy' – Roxy Music
'Lazy Sunday' – The Small Faces
'Me Myself And I' – De La Soul
'Patience' – Guns 'N' Roses
'Sitting On The Dock Of The Bay' – Otis Redding
'Wind Of Change' – The Scorpions

— MULLET OVER: THE WORST HAIRCUTS IN ROCK —

The Mullet
The worst haircut of the 1980s – as seen on artists who really should have known better, such as Bono from U2 – persists to this day, largely in the style vacuum that is football. A haircut for the terminally indecisive, the mullet is long at the back but short at the top and sides. Nowadays, sometimes worn ironically.

Elton's head
Although not strictly a haircut – Elton's barnet is attached to his head using medical trickery – Elton John's hair is a constant source of grim fascination for aficionados of rock hair-styles: 'You mean, he paid to look like that?'.

The Flock of Seagulls
This early '80s band would be utterly forgotten if it weren't for one thing: former hairdresser Mike Score's sloping haircut, which made him look like a startled goose.

The Dave Hill
It's difficult to single out one glam rocker when you consider the fashion atrocities of the time, but Slade's Dave Hill stands out for his enthusiastic adoption of the bowl cut.

The Hoxton Fin
Travis's Fran Healy was one of many pop stars who adopted the fin, a kind of Mohican for people too embarrassed to get a proper punk haircut. Inevitably, David Beckham sported one too.

The Limahl
The Kajagoogoo frontman's hair was as bizarre as his band's name. Thanks to gel and dye, the singer went out in public looking as if someone had dropped a half-eaten fish supper on his head.

The Brian May
For years, rock fans looked at Queen guitarist Brian May's bouffant perm and thought 'he reminds me of someone'. Then May teamed up with *EastEnders'* Anita Dobson and the cry of 'it's twins!' rang out across the land.

— THE BIG FIVE —

In 2004, just five giant record companies dominated the world of music – and two of them, Sony and BMG, announced their plans to merge.

The big five were:

BMG Entertainment
EMI Group
Sony Music Entertainment
Universal Music Group
Warner Brothers Music

— THE HORROR, THE HORROR —

10 novelty songs that still give us nightmares...

'Achy Breaky Heart' – Billy Ray Cyrus (1992)
'Agadoo' – Black Lace (1984)
'Fog On The Tyne' – Gazza & Lindisfarne (1990)
'Itsy Witsy Teeny Weeny Yellow Polka Dot Bikini'
– Bombalurina feat. Timmy Mallett (1991)
'Mr Blobby' – Mr Blobby (1993)
'Orville's Song' – Keith Harris & Orville (1980)
'Shaddap You Face' – Joe Dolce (1981)
'The Birdie Song' – The Tweets (1981)
'There's No-One Quite Like Grandma'
– St Winifred's School Choir (1980)
'Y Viva Espana' – Sylvia (1974)

— THE WIT AND WISDOM OF THE GALLAGHERS —
PART TWO

'He was in Take That! He's a fat dancer from Take That. Somebody who danced for a living. Stick to what you're good at, that's what I always say.'
Noel on Robbie Williams, *Heat* Magazine

'They should be shot.'
Noel on the Backstreet Boys, speaking to *dotmusic*

— MUSICIANS' AILMENTS —

It's not just heroin addiction and alcoholism that plague musicians: many of them go under the surgeon's knife for life-saving surgery, while others suffer from assorted aches and pains.

Adam Ant	Manic depression
Ann Wilson (Heart)	Underwent weight-loss surgery in 2002
Beth Orton	Suffers from Crohn's Disease
Britney Spears	Underwent knee surgery in 2004
Courtney Love	Hospitalised due to a 'gynaecological condition' in 2004
David Bowie	Underwent emergency heart surgery in 2004
Elton John	Had nodules removed from his vocal cords in 1986
Jonny Greenwood (Radiohead)	Repetitive strain injury in right arm
Meat Loaf	Underwent heart surgery in 2003
Robbie Williams	Admits to depression
Anastacia	Survived breast cancer

— PRETENTIOUS? MOI? —
PART ONE

'People really lead flat lives. They need some sort of peak. I like to be that peak.'
Michael Hutchence, INXS

'We want to be the band to dance to when the bomb drops.'
Simon Le Bon, Duran Duran

'I do my best work when I'm in pain and turmoil.'
Sting

'I am interested in anything about revolt, disorder, chaos – especially activity that seems to have no meaning. It seems to me to be the road toward freedom... Rather than starting inside, I start outside and reach the mental through the physical.'
Jim Morrison, The Doors

'When we separate music from life we get art.'
John Cage

— ROCK STAR RIDERS —

The rider – the food, drink and other items provided by a venue when a band comes to town – is an essential part of any gig, and some bands take their requests to extremes: Van Halen famously asked for a bowl of M&M chocolates with all the brown ones removed. The request isn't as daft as it sounds, though: as the urban legends site *snopes.com* points out, if the band arrived and discovered brown M&Ms, it suggested that the concert promoter hadn't bothered reading the fine print of the contract. As David Lee Roth explained in his autobiography: 'So, when I would walk backstage, if I saw a brown M&M in that bowl... guaranteed you're going to arrive at a technical error. They didn't read the contract. Guaranteed you'd run into a problem. Sometimes it would threaten to just destroy the whole show. Something like, literally, life-threatening.' In one case, a venue that provided brown M&Ms hadn't checked the weight requirements, and the weight of the stage was too much for the venue floor. The stage sank, causing thousands of dollars of damage to the venue.

Not all rider requests are as sensible, though. Limp Bizkit demand 'dimmable lamps'; Jennifer Lopez demands a white room with white flowers, white tables, white candles and white couches; Britney Spears wants a 'clean and odour free carpeted or rugged floor' and a telephone, with a fine of $5,000 for any incoming calls; INXS demanded a table tennis table; and Def Leppard want to know the radio frequencies of every police, ambulance and fire engine in the area to make sure their signals won't interfere with the band's wireless guitars. When the band's on stage, they also demand that all mobile phones, pagers and walkie-talkies used by police and other authorities are switched off.

— THREE STEPS TO HEAVEN —

As '50s rocker Eddie Cochran sang, there are three steps to Heaven. As life travels on and things do go wrong, just follow steps one, two and three:

Step 1: You find a girl you love
Step 2: She falls in love with you
Step 3: You kiss and hold her tightly

— THE ROCK CALENDAR

'January' – Elton John
'February Stars' – Foo Fighters
'Death March' – Faith No More
'April Skies' – Jesus and Mary Chain
'Maggie May' – Rod Stewart
'June' – Pete Yorn
'July' – Dashboard Confessional
'August And Everything After' – Counting Crows
'Pale September' – Fiona Apple
'October' – U2
'November Rain' – Guns 'N' Roses
'December' – Teenage Fanclub

— LIVE AID —

On 13 July 1985, anyone who was anyone in the world of rock and pop played at *Live Aid*, the biggest charity concert the world has ever seen. However, while we all remember U2 and Queen, how many of us can recall the performances by such giants as Nik Kershaw and Yu Rock Mission? Here's the full *Live Aid* line-up in order of appearance.

Live Aid UK

Status Quo
The Style Council
The Boomtown Rats
Adam Ant
[From Australia: INXS, Dragon, Men At Work, Little River Band, Gowana]
Ultravox
[From Japan: Loudness, Off Cause, Eikichi Yazawa, Motoharu Sano]
Spandau Ballet
Elvis Costello
[From Austria: Austria For Afrika]
Nik Kershaw
[From Holland: BB King]
Sade
[From Yugoslavia: Yu Rock Mission]
Sting and Phil Collins

Howard Jones
[From Russia: Avtograf]
Bryan Ferry
[From Germany: Band Fur Afrika]
Paul Young & Alison Moyet
U2
Dire Straits
Queen
David Bowie & Mick Jagger
David Bowie
The Who
Elton John
Elton John & Kiki Dee
Elton John, George Michael & Andrew Ridgeley
Freddie Mercury & Brian May
Paul McCartney
Grand finale

Live Aid USA

Bernard Watson
Joan Baez
The Hooters
The Four Tops
Billy Ocean
Black Sabbath
Run DMC
Rick Springfield
REO Speedwagon feat. The Beach Boys
Crosby, Stills & Nash
Judas Priest
Bryan Adams
The Beach Boys
George Thorogood & The Destroyers, feat. Bo Diddley and Albert Collins
Simple Minds
The Pretenders
Santana, feat. Pat Metheny
Ashford & Simpson
Kool & The Gang (video)
Madonna
Tom Petty & The Heartbreakers
Kenny Loggins
The Cars
Neil Young
The Power Station
Thompson Twins
Eric Clapton
Phil Collins
Led Zeppelin
Crosby Stills Nash & Young
Duran Duran
Patti Labelle
Hall & Oates feat. Eddie Kendricks & David Ruffin
Mick Jagger & Tina Turner
Bob Dylan, Ron Wood & Keith Richards
Finale

Source: www.live-aid.info

— TAT'S ENTERTAINMENT: TATTOOS OF THE STARS — PART TWO

Kurt Cobain
K Records logo on arm

Jonathan Davis (Korn)
HIV on left shoulder, KORN logo on back, bishop ripping his skin off to reveal Jesus on right bicep

Eminem
Dog tags around neck, large mushroom on left shoulder, right inside arm has daughter's name (Hailie Jade), gothic style bracelet on left wrist, 'Slit Here' on right wrist, D on right forearm, 12 on left forearm, one tattoo standing for Eminem on one side of chest, one tattoo standing for Slim Shady on the other side, design on right bicep

— EAT TO THE BEAT —

On the face of it, there are thousands of songs about food: Kelis sings about her milk shake, John Lennon had a thing for cold turkey, and Booker T And The MGs played 'Green Onions'. On closer investigation, though, very few songs are about food at all. Food is used as an analogy – 'Life is a minestrone' – or as slang – 'Cold Turkey' – and more often than not, as a euphemism. Prince and Kelis may have sang about cream and milkshakes respectively, but you can be pretty sure that neither of them had dairy produce on their mind.

The tradition of using food as a euphemism goes back to the days of blues, where singers managed to create utterly filthy songs that sounded perfectly innocuous thanks to the use of food terms – jelly rolls, squeezing lemons and so on. It's a tradition brought right up to date by South Park's Chef, who urged listeners to 'suck on my chocolate salty balls'. The following list contains some analogies, some slang and of course, plenty of songs about sex.

'Breakfast In America' – Supertramp
'Chocolate Cake' – Crowded House
'Chocolate Salty Balls' – Chef (South Park)
'Cold Turkey' – John Lennon
'Cream' – Prince
'Eat For Two' – 10,000 Maniacs
'Eat To The Beat' – Blondie
'Green Onions' – Booker T And The MGs
'Life Is A Minestrone' – 10CC
'Mayonnaise' – Smashing Pumpkins
'Milkshake' – Kelis
'Peaches' – Presidents Of The USA
'Rock Lobster' – B-52s
'Snack Attack' – Godley & Crème
'Sugar And Spice' – The Searchers
'The Coffee Song' – Frank Sinatra

— THE WORLD'S MOST RECORDED SONG —

According to Guinness World Records, the world's most recorded song is Paul McCartney's 'Yesterday', which was recorded some 1,600 times between 1965 and 1986. Artists who have covered 'Yesterday' include Elvis, Sinatra, James Brown and Gladys Knight, and the song is still the most played record on radio stations around the world.

— MUSICIANS AND THEIR GOOD CAUSES —

Asian Dub Foundation	Miscarriage of justice (Satpal Ram)
Beastie Boys	Human rights in Tibet
Billy Bragg	Socialism
Chrissie Hynde	Animal rights
Coldplay	Fair Trade
George Harrison	Floods in Bangladesh
John Lennon	Peace movement
Live Aid	Famine
Neil Young	The Bridge School, San Francisco
Paul McCartney	September 11th charities
Robbie Williams	Testicular cancer
Sting	Environmentalism
Ted Nugent	Libertarianism
Tom Robinson	Gay rights
U2	Third world debt, AIDS

— DESERT ISLAND DISCS —

Since 1942, Radio 4's *Desert Island Discs* has invited the great and good to select the eight records they would take with them to a desert island. Some of the choices have been interesting...

Ian Duncan Smith (Tory)	'My City Of Ruins', Bruce Springsteen
Charles Kennedy (Lib Dem)	'Young Americans', David Bowie
Nigella Lawson (celebrity chef)	'Cleaning Out My Closet', Eminem
Brian May (ex-Queen)	'To Know Him Is To Love Him', Anita Dobson feat. Brian May; 'We Will Rock You', Queen
Robin Cook (Labour)	'Mr Tambourine Man', Bob Dylan
George Foreman (boxer)	'Mama Said Knock You Out', LL Cool J
George Clooney (actor)	'Lucy In The Sky With Diamonds', William Shatner
Paul Whitehouse (comedian)	'God Save The Queen', Sex Pistols

— GRAVE NEWS: ROCKERS EPITAPHS —

Despite the fact that Kurt Cobain's ashes are said to have been scattered, widow Courtney Love claims that her house has become a shrine, so much so that she has had to install 24 hour security so that the fans 'won't come to my f***ing house'. She reportedly plans a memorial containing an epitaph from 'Dumb': 'I'm not like them but I can pretend/The sun is gone but I have a light/The day is done but I'm having fun.'

One suitably remote option would be the Per la Chaise cemetary in Paris, which famously hosts the final resting place of departed Doors mainman Jim Morrison. Following the theft of two plaques – both, curiously, misspelled as 'Morisson, James Douglas' – a bronze plaque was eventually attached more firmly to the grave. It bears the Greek inscription KATA TON DAIMONA EAYTOY meaning 'to the divine spirit within himself', although different translations could be made: 'The devil within himself', 'The genius in his mind', or even 'He caused his own demons'.

24-hour security is in place at Gracelands, where Elvis Presley's grave includes a 20-line eulogy written by his father, which starts: 'He was a precious gift from God / We cherished and loved dearly'.

Jimi Hendrix's grave bears the more succinct 'Forever in our hearts' while Joy Division frontman Ian Curtis's grave is inscribed with the song title that became his epitaph – 'Love Will Tear Us Apart'.

— GIRLS AGAINST BOYS —

Biggest-selling single by a female group	The Spice Girls, 'Wannabe'
Fastest selling pop album of all time	N'Sync, *No Strings Attached*
Highest ever annual earnings by a girl band	The Spice Girls, £29.6 million (1998)
Most consecutive Christmas number ones	The Spice Girls*
Most expensive pop star clothing	Geri Halliwell's union jack dress, sold for £41,320

* A record matched only by The Beatles
Source: Guinness World Records

— WORKING TITLES —

A Doll's House – The Beatles, *The White Album*
Don't Be A Faggot – Beastie Boys, *License To Ill*
Eclipse – Pink Floyd, *Dark Side Of The Moon*
Emotional Fascism – Elvis Costello, *Armed Forces*
Everyone Wants To Shag The Teardrop Explodes – The Teardrop
Explodes, *Kilimanjaro*
Exploding Head – REM, *Monster*
Get Back – The Beatles, *Let It Be*
Margaret On The Guillotine – The Smiths, *The Queen Is Dead*
Metal Up Your Ass – Metallica, *Kill 'Em All*
Ones And Zeroes – Radiohead, *OK Computer*
The Deaf, Dumb And Blind Boy – The Who, *Tommy*
U2, Love Your Early Stuff – U2, *The Best Of 1980 – 1990*

— DANCE GENRES – A BRIEF GUIDE —
PART ONE

It seems that there are as many genres of dance music as there are artists, and many genres have baffling names: can you tell the difference between trance, Goa trance and progressive trance? If you want to be a real dance geek, you'll need to know the following – and stay up to date: new genres seem to appear every day.

Ambient: Music designed to surround you without drawing attention to itself
Ambient groove: Ambient music with added beats
Breakbeat hardcore: Acid house with hip-hop influences
Chemical breaks: Combines rock, hip-hop and house
Drum and bass: Reggae basslines and hip-hop/techno beats
Drill and bass: Offshoot of drum and bass featuring very fast snare drum rolls
Jungle: Fast (up to 190 bpm) music with heavy basslines and a mix-and-match of styles
Downtempo: Laid-back electronic music designed for listening, not dancing, to
Nu Jazz: Combination of electronic music and jazz
Trip-hop: Downtempo, jazzy dance music popularised by Portishead, Massive Attack etc.
Electro: Music influenced by Kraftwerk and funk: think Africa Bambaataa's 'Planet Rock'

— FIRST EVER UK DOWNLOAD CHART —

In 2004, the British record industry announced that it would start an official UK download chart on 1 September – but three months before, it released test data that effectively formed the first ever Top 20 for digital downloads.

Position	Title	Artist
1.	Pixies	'Bam Thwok'
2.	Maroon	'This Love'
3.	Outkast	'Hey Ya!'
4.	Anastacia	'Left Outside Alone'
5.	Mario Winans	'I Don't Wanna Know'
6.	The Corrs	'Summer Sunshine'
7.	Rasmus	'In The Shadows'
8.	Keane	'Everybody's Changing'
9.	Jet	'Are You Gonna Be My Girl'
10.	Beastie Boys	'Ch-Check It Out'
11.	George Michael	'Flawless'
12.	The Streets	'Dry Your Eyes'
13.	Britney Spears	'Everytime'
14.	Avril Lavigne	'Don't Tell Me'
15.	The Streets	'Fit But You Know It'
16.	Dido	'White Flag'
17.	The Cure	'Lost'
18.	Snow Patrol	'Run'
19.	Keane	'Somewhere Only We Know'
20.	Ash	'Teenage Kicks'

— CLASSICAL ROCK —

Tunes that 'borrow' from the great classical composers:

The Beach Boys – 'Lady Linda': based on Dvořák's 'Pie Jesu'
Manfred Mann – 'Joybringer': based on Holst's 'Mars' from *The Planets*
Sky – 'Toccata': based on Bach's 'Toccata And Fugue'
Emerson, Lake and Palmer – 'Tarkus': borrows parts of Bach's 'Toccata in F and Prelude VI'.
Emerson, Lake and Palmer – 'Trilogy': includes elements of Aaron Copland's 'Rodeo'
Emerson, Lake and Palmer – 'Toccata': an adaptation of Ginastera's *1st Piano Concerto*, 4th movement

— YOU'VE COME A LONG WAY, BABY —

Rock megastars' more modest beginnings...

Coldplay: They may be filling stadiums today, but the band's first gig in 1998 was at the rather less impressive Laurel Tree in London's Camden. And they were called Starfish.

Franz Ferdinand: According to their official record company biography, Franz Ferdinand's first gig was in a friend's bedroom in 2001.

Metallica: Way back in 1982, Metallica's first show was in Anaheim, California. Writing in his diary, drummer Lars Ulrich wrote: 'First gig ever. Very nervous. Only band. Dave broke a string on the first song. Played so-so! Went down pretty good. Crowd ca.75. Pay $15.'

Oasis: The band's first show, in 1991 at Manchester's Boardwalk, didn't feature Noel Gallagher: although he was present, he didn't join his brother's band until 1992.

Radiohead: Thom Yorke, Colin Greenwood and Ed O'Brien's first gig together was a teenage friend's birthday party in 1982

REM: REM's first gig – as The Twisted Kites – was at a party in a church in Athens, Georgia.

U2: The band's first London gig in 1979 attracted just nine people.

— ROCK OFFSPRING: KILL YOUR PARENTS! —

Apple (Chris Martin, Coldplay)
Blue Angel (The Edge, U2)
Dandelion (Keith Richards)
Dweezil (Frank Zappa)
Fifi Trixibelle (Bob Geldof)
Heavenly Hiraani Tiger Lily (Michael Hutchence)
Jermajesty (Jermaine Jackson)
Moon Unit (Frank Zappa)
Peaches (Bob Geldof)
Prince Michael (Michael Jackson)
Ross (Diana Ross)
Zowie (David Bowie)

— STORMIN' NORMAN —
The Amazing Adventures of Fatboy Slim

1963	Born in Bromley and named Quentin Cook
1986	Now named Norman, becomes bassist with The Housemartins
1988	The Housemartins split up; Norman begins his remixing career
1989	Releases 'Won't Talk About It' featuring Billy Bragg
1990	Formed Beats International; begins remixing other artists' records
1991	Disbanded Beats International; formed Freakpower
1993	Begins recording under various aliases: Pizzaman, the Mighty Dub Katz, Fried Funk Food
1995	Invents the alias Fatboy Slim as 'a fun side project'
1997	Releases the first Fatboy Slim album, *Better Living Through Chemistry*
1998	Releases *You've Come A Long Way, Baby* and becomes a regular in the charts
2000	Releases *Halfway Between The Gutter And The Stars*; the Christopher Walken-starring video for 'Weapon Of Choice' picks up a Grammy and six MTV Music Video Awards
2001	Plays on Brighton Beach to an estimated crowd of 35,000
2002	Returns to Brighton and plays to an incredible 250,000
2004	Releases the fourth Fatboy Slim album, *Palookaville*

— CHECK THE MIKE —

John Otway's sets often featured major microphone abuse, including headbutting during the song 'Headbutts'. He gained a sponsorship deal with Shure, which was terminated when Otway managed to destroy a SM58 while journalists were there to witness it.

Julian Cope improvised with a broken stand, mutilating his stomach with the sharp edges during a performance of 'Reynard The Fox'. Eventually he built one which was so indestructible that he could climb and swing from it. In 1993 he raised over £2,500 for anti-fur campaigners Lynx by raffling it.

Before Queen had even formed Freddie Mercury got fed up with a big heavy stand and thus took it apart, forming the 3-foot largely useless sawn-off affair that became his trademark (along with the 'tache).

— DON'T GET ON THAT PLANE! —

The Wright Brothers have a lot to answer for. Apart from enabling Phil Collins to torture the world TWICE in one day for *Live Aid*, they are also responsible for some of the greatest losses in the world of popular music.

The roll call includes:
Glenn Miller
Buddy Holly
The Big Bopper
Ritchie Vallens
Patsy Cline
Jim Reeves
Otis Redding
Jim Croce
Ronnie Van Zant & Steve Gaines (Lynyrd Skynyrd)
Ricky Nelson
John Denver
Aaliyah

Plane crash survivors are, unsurprisingly, in shorter supply, apart from the rest of Lynyrd Skynyrd. However, the god of flying preserved Gary Numan – who merely crash-landed his own light aircraft – and Waylon Jennings, who gave up his seat on the ill-fated Buddy Holly flight.

— ART FOR ART'S SAKE —

Ten musicians who've tried their hand at art:

David Bowie: Painting
Ronnie Wood: Painting
Paul McCartney: Painting
Bryan Adams: Fashion photography
Holly Johnson: Painting
Ian Dury: Painting
Paul Simonon (The Clash): Painting
Joni Mitchell: Painting
Michael Stipe: Photography
Bono: Illustrating children's books

— TEN WEDDING FAVOURITES —

1. '(Everything I Do) I Do It For You' – Bryan Adams
2. 'We Have All The Time In The World' – Louis Armstrong
3. 'It Has To Be You' – Harry Connick, Jr
4. 'When A Man Loves A Woman' – Percy Sledge
5. 'Have I Told You Lately' – Rod Stewart
6. 'Wonderful Tonight' – Eric Clapton
7. 'Love Is All Around' – Wet Wet Wet
8. 'Let's Stay Together' – Al Green
9. 'My Girl' – Temptations
10. 'Unchained Melody' – Righteous Brothers

— THE FIRST GLASTONBURY FESTIVAL —

The inaugural Glastonbury took place from 19–20 September, 1970, at Pilton Farm and was inspired by the Bath Blues Festival. For the £1 entry fee (including free milk from organiser Michael Eavis's cows), 1500 people enjoyed acts including Marc Bolan and T-Rex (Bolan arriving in a velvet-covered car), Al Stewart, Steamhammer, Quintessence and Ian Anderson (no, not the Jethro Tull flautist).

The Kinks pulled out, and the event was overshadowed by the death of Jimi Hendrix the day before. Despite Eavis predicting that the event was 'the quickest way of clearing my overdraft', he still lost £1,500.

— TALLEST AND SHORTEST —

Tiny Tim was 6' 1". Another myth shattered.

Tallest
Long John Baldry: 6' 7"
Krist Noveselic (bass player for Nirvana): 6' 7"
Peter Steele (singer for Type O Negative): 6' 6"
Mick Fleetwood: 6' 5"

Shortest
Edith Piaf: 4' 8"
Paula Abdul: 5' 1"
Sam Fox: 5' 1"
Prince: 5' 2"

— THE WORST GIG EVER? —

Industrial art-rockers Einsturzende Neubauten's mid-'80s finale was to chuck a load of bottles in a cement mixer. The ensuing explosion showered the audience with broken glass and almost sparked a riot.

Throbbing Gristle's live acts were a legendary onslaught of noise and disturbing imagery. During a show at the London Film-Makers Co-op an audience member went into spontaneous orgasm, apparently triggered by something in the music. Singer Genesis P Orridge commented 'because we keep a cassette of each gig... we could have worked out exactly what sounds made it happen... I was trying desperately to find out exactly at what point in the concert it had happened.'

The Jesus And Mary Chain's early gigs have become the stuff of legend. not just because their screeching feedback was so unbearable, but rather because their 15 minute sets – during which they only faced the crowd to goad them, guitars up against the amps – were so enjoyed by the audience that riots were commonplace at their shows.

Sometimes the audience give as good as they get. Bonnie Tyler was bottled mercilessly by rock fans at Reading in 1988, as was ex-pat and Prince/Esther Rantzen protégé Sheena Easton when she returned to Glasgow Green sporting a brand new mid-Atlantic accent.

The Everly Brothers split publicly and emphatically, in 1973. At Knott's Berry Farm (an amusement park gig) Don got trashed, picked a fight with Phil and destroyed his guitar.

— 11 FILMS NAMED AFTER SONGS —

Boogie Nights (1997) – Heatwave
Dazed And Confused (1993) – Led Zeppelin
Less Than Zero (1987) – Elvis Costello
Man On The Moon (1999) – REM
My Own Private Idaho (1991) – The B-52s
Pretty In Pink (1986) – Psychedelic Furs
Pretty Woman (1990) – Roy Orbison
Strange Days (1995) – The Doors
The Crying Game (1992) – Dave Berry
What's Love Got To Do With It (1993) – Tina Turner
When a Man Loves A Woman (1994) – Percy Sledge

— BACKMASKING —

Do records really contain secret backwards messages?

The controversy over backmasking – messages that are only audible when you play a record backwards – has raged for years, with some notable allegations:

Led Zeppelin, 'Stairway To Heaven'
'Here's to my sweet Satan. The one whose little path would make me sad, whose power is Satan. He'll give you 555, there was a little toolshed where he made us suffer, sad Satan'

The Beatles, *The White Album*
'Paul is dead, man, miss him, miss him'

The Eagles, 'Hotel California'
'Satan, he organised his own religion, well he knows he should, so nice it was delicious, it cooks it in a vat he fixed for his son whom he gives away'

Judas Priest, 'Better By You Better Than Me'
'Do it'

'Twinkle Twinkle Little Star'
'I wish there was no Allah'

While most such claims are nonsense – as Judas Priest pointed out, urging fans to kill themselves didn't make financial sense; they'd be better leaving messages saying 'buy more of our records' – some backmasking does exist:

Roger Waters put a backwards message on 'Empty Spaces' (on *The Wall*) saying 'Congratulations, you've just discovered the secret message. Please send your answer to old Pink, care of the funny farm, Chatford'; ELO's 'Fire On High' has a message saying 'The music is reversible but time is not – turn back! Turn back! Turn back!'; and Christian rockers Petra recorded a message on their song 'Judas Kiss' that said: 'What are you looking for the devil for, when you ought to be looking for the Lord?'

— FIVE WAYS TO LEAVE YOUR LOVER —

Paul Simon may have sung that there were 50 ways to leave your lover, but he only listed five:

1. Slip out the back, Jack
2. Make a new plan, Stan
3. You don't need to be coy, Roy, just set yourself free
4. Hop on the bus, Gus
5. Drop off the key, Lee

— DON'T JUDGE AN ALBUM BY ITS COVER —

Famous album cover designers:

Peter Saville: Responsible for Factory Records' entire output – including Joy Division's albums and singles, New Order's 'Blue Monday' floppy disc sleeve plus Suede, Eno, Roxy Music, Ultravox, Goldie, Pulp and even Paul McCartney and Wham

Malcolm Garrett: Under the name Assorted Images created cut-and-paste punk and new wave sleeves for Buzzcocks, then Culture Club, Duran Duran and Simple Minds

Hipgnosis: Classic '70s albums like Led Zeppelin's *Houses Of The Holy*, *Wish You Were Here* by Pink Floyd, and albums by Styx and Scorpions

Mark Farrow: Pet Shop Boys and Spiritualised

Jamie Reid: Sex Pistols designer, best known for putting a safety pin through the Queen's nose

Roger Dean: Synonymous with the sleeves of Yes

Vaughan Oliver: Designed most of 4AD's sleeves – Frank Black, Pixies, Cocteau Twins, This Mortal Coil plus Robert Fripp and David Sylvian

Neville Brody: Now known as a magazine designer (*The Face*) and typographer, he also worked on covers for Cabaret Voltaire and 23 Skidoo

Joni Mitchell: Painted the majority of her album covers

— LONGEST AND SHORTEST —

In the good old days of vinyl an album was limited to around 25 minutes a side, so the longest albums stretched on to double and triple albums (usually with gatefold artwork by Roger Dean). Lou Reed's *Metal Machine Music* was only a double, but seemed to last forever.

In the CD era multi-disc albums are even longer – notable examples being the Magnetic Fields' *69 Songs* and Prince's *Emancipation*. Merzbow's *Merzbox* is 50 CDs long, though it is largely a compilation box-set. There's also Throbbing Gristle's *24 Hours*, which was originally released as 24 C60 cassettes but is now available on Mute Records as the same number of hour-long CDs.

However, nothing can beat John Cage's piece 'Slow As Possible', which lasts 639 years. CD release plans are unconfirmed at time of going to press.

For the shortest record of all time we are in a grey area, and that's before we consider the *Best Of Westlife*. When does an album become an EP, or mini-album?

Two of the shortest albums in the days of 12" vinyl both came from the '60s – the Dave Clark Five's *Try Too Hard* and the Electric Prunes' *Mass In F Minor* both clocked in at under 20 minutes, half the length of your average Orb single.

Really pushing the boundaries of what makes an album are the compilations put out by Scottish independent Stereo Solution. *The Littlest Albums* (standing at two volumes and counting) each contain 12 tracks – six per side – on a 7" single. That surely is a record?

— TIME SIGNATURES —

Song	Artist	Time Signature
'Golden Brown'	The Stranglers	13/8 and 3/4
'Living In The Past'	Jethro Tull	5/4
'Take 5'	Dave Brubeck	5/4
'Good Morning'	The Beatles	5/4
'Seven Days'	Sting	5/4
'Everybody Hurts'	REM	6/8
'Money'	Pink Floyd	7/4
'Love Is Stronger Than Justice'	Sting	7/8

— THE BEST GUITAR RIFFS IN THE WORLD... EVER! —

1. 'Sweet Child O' Mine' – Guns 'N' Roses
2. 'Smells Like Teen Spirit' – Nirvana
3. 'Whole Lotta Love' – Led Zeppelin
4. 'Smoke On The Water' – Deep Purple
5. 'Enter Sandman' – Metallica
6. 'Layla' – Derek & The Dominos/Eric Clapton
7. 'Master Of Puppets' – Metallica
8. 'Back In Black' – AC/DC
9. 'Voodoo Chile (Slight Return)' – Jimi Hendrix
10. 'Paranoid' – Black Sabbath
11. 'Crazy Train' – Ozzy Osbourne
12. 'All Right Now' – Free
13. 'Plug In Baby' – Muse
14. 'Black Dog' – Led Zeppelin
15. 'Ain't Talkin' 'Bout Love' – Van Halen
16. 'Walk This Way' – Aerosmith and Run DMC
17. 'Sunshine Of Your Love' – Cream
18. 'No One Knows' – Queens Of The Stone Age
19. 'Paradise City' – Guns 'N' Roses
20. 'Killing In The Name' – Rage Against The Machine

— *BE HERE NOW*: THE COVER EXPLAINED —

The cover of *Be Here Now* is Oasis's *Sergeant Pepper*, and it's packed with objects. According to fan sites, the items have particular meanings:

Clock: reference to the station clock in *A Hard Day's Night*
Globe and telescope: homage to a scene from *Magical Mystery Tour*; also refers to the song 'All Around The World'
House: a favourite hangout of Who drummer Keith Moon
Car: a copy of John Lennon's car, and a tribute to Moon's penchant for driving cars into pools
Calendar: The album's release date
Scooter: Reference to '60s mod culture
White TV: Resembles the TV in The Who's *Tommy*
Gramophone: Associated with HMV, The Beatles' original record label
Parking Meter: Reference to The Beatles' 'Lovely Rita'
Phone Box: Paul McCartney hid in one in *A Hard Day's Night*

Then again, they may be wrong. Speaking to *Q* Magazine, designer Brian Cannon explained: 'None of it really meant anything.'.

— THE MAN VS THE KIDS —

In 2003, the Recording Industry Association of America (RIAA) cracked down on 'music pirates', taking legal action against 261 users of file sharing software. It was just the first in an onslaught of legal attacks: by February, the RIAA had taken action against 1,445 people and negotiated 381 settlements. By June 2004, the number of people sued by the recording industry had reached 3,429, with at least 600 of the accused settling for around $3,000 each. At the time of writing, the UK equivalent of the RIAA – the British Phonographic Industry (BPI) – hasn't adopted similar tactics, although it hasn't ruled them out either.

Statistics suggest that the lawsuits have had little effect on the amount of music being shared on the Internet, but they have resulted in a flood of bad PR for the RIAA. One $300m lawsuit had to be abandoned after the supposed music pirate turned out to be a 66-year-old woman who'd never seen a file sharing program in her life, while another action forced the parent of a 12-year-old schoolgirl to pay $2,000 to the record industry.

— BAD SPORTS —

Sportsmen who want to be rock stars

Alex Higgins: Released novelty single 'One-Four-Seven' in 1980
Andy Cole: Released an R&B track in 1999. It bombed
Eddie The Eagle: Reached number 2 in Finland with 'Mun Niemi En Eetu' (My Name Is Eddie)
Gazza: Teamed up with Lindisfarne for 1990 number 2, 'Fog On The Tyne'
Glenn Hoddle & Chris Waddle: Reached number 12 with 'Diamond Lights' in 1987
John Barnes: Rapped – badly – on New Order's 1990 football theme 'World In Motion'
Kevin Keegan: Reached the lower reaches of the charts with 'Head Over Heels In Love' in 1976
Pat Cash & John McEnroe: Released a charity single with members of Iron Maiden in 1991
Ron Atkinson: Released a Christmas single in 2003
Terry Venables: Released 'What Do You Want To Make Those Eyes At Me For' in 1974. It wasn't a big success
Vinnie Jones: Released an album in 2002

— LONGEST GAP BETWEEN NUMBER ONE HITS —

George Harrison's 'My Sweet Lord' was first a number 1 in January 1971. A few weeks after his death – 31 years later – it returned to the top, in January 2002.

The longest gap between number 1s with different tracks belongs to The Righteous Brothers (25 years 8 months). In Feb 1965 'You've Lost That Lovin' Feeling' was number 1, as was 'Unchained Melody' in 1990.

The longest gap between chart-topping non re-releases is 18 years and 3 months for Blondie (from Nov 1980, 'The Tide Is High', to Feb 1999, 'Maria').

— ON THE FIDDLE —

Nigel Kennedy (spiky-haired Vivaldi-pedlar also known for nicking Mark E Smith's missus) isn't the sole contributor to the world of contemporary violin use. There are many more songs featuring the 4-stringed wonder:

Electric Light Orchestra –'10538 Overture'
The epitome of classical and rock cross-over, with a small string section on every one of their hits

Violinski – 'Clog Dance'
Solo effort from ex-ELO stringsman Mik Kaminski

Velvet Underground – 'Venus In Furs'
OK, OK, so John Cale was actually playing a viola...

Billy Bragg – 'You Woke Up My Neighbourhood'
The bard of Barking gets some culture

Other honorable mentions:
Slade – 'Coz I Luv You'
Levellers – 'Beautiful Day'
Dexy's Midnight Runners – 'Come On Eileen'

— THE FIRST *TOP OF THE POPS* LINEUP —

Presented by Jimmy Saville on 1 January 1964

The Rolling Stones – 'I Wanna Be Your Man'
Dusty Springfield – 'I Only Wanna Be With You'
The Dave Clark Five – 'Glad All Over'
The Hollies – 'Stay'
The Swinging Blue Jeans – 'Hippy Hippy Shake'

Discs and filmed items
Cliff Richard and The Shadows – 'Wonderful Life'
Freddie And The Dreamers – 'You Were Made For Me'
Gene Pitney – 'Twenty-Four Hours From Tulsa'

Plus Beatles news clips ('I Wanna Hold Your Hand')

— THE KIDS ARE ALL WIGHT —

The Isle Of Wight festival ran for three years. Initially set up as a swimming pool fund-raiser, the 1968 lineup included:

The Pretty Things, Arthur Brown (Fire) and Jefferson Airplane, The Move, Marc Bolan and Steve Took (aka Tyrannosaurus Rex) and Fairport Convention. It was a one-day event – well, from 6pm-1am – compered by John Peel.

In 1969 the event was expanded to three days, starting on 29th August, and featured The Bonzo Dog Doo-Dah Band, The Nice, Richie Havens, Bob Dylan and The Band, Blodwyn Pig, Edgar Broughton Band, The Pretty Things, Family, Free, The Who, Joe Cocker and The Moody Blues.

In 1970 the festival ran for five days from August 26th. The bill included many artists appearing more than once and featured: Kris Kristofferson, Supertramp, Gilberto Gil, Family, Procol Harum, Joni Mitchell, Tiny Tim, Miles Davis, Ten Years After, Emerson, Lake and Palmer, The Doors, The Who, Melanie, Sly And The Family Stone. Ralph McTell, Free, Donovan, The Moody Blues, Jethro Tull, Jimi Hendrix, Joan Baez, Leonard Cohen and Richie Havens. (Jimi Hendrix died 18 days later.)

— WHERE IN THE WORLD? —

Album cover	Artist	Location
Abbey Road	The Beatles	Abbey Road, London
Animals	Pink Floyd	Battersea Power Station, London
Hotel California	The Eagles	Beverly Hills Hotel, Los Angeles
Houses Of The Holy	Led Zeppelin	The Giant's Causeway, Northern Ireland
London Calling	The Clash	The Palladium, New York
Morrison Hotel	The Doors	Los Angeles
Physical Graffiti	Led Zeppelin	St Mark's Place, New York
The Joshua Tree	U2	Joshua Tree National Park, Mojave Desert, US
The Unforgettable Fire	U2	Slane Castle, Co. Meath, Ireland
What's The Story...	Oasis	Berwick Street, Soho, London
Who's Next	The Who	A slag heap, somewhere in England

— THE HIT FACTORY —

Between 1984 and 1993 production team Stock, Aitken and Waterman's knack for matching perky performers with perfect pop music racked up hundreds of hits, including 13 number 1s. The chart toppers were:

'You Spin Me Round' – Dead Or Alive
'Respectable' – Mel & Kim
'Let It Be' – Ferry Aid
'Never Gonna Give You Up' – Rick Astley
'I Should Be So Lucky' – Kylie Minogue
'Especially For You' – Kylie & Jason
'Too Many Broken Hearts' – Jason Donovan
'Hand On Your Heart' – Kylie Minogue
'Ferry Cross The Mersey' – Various
'Sealed With A Kiss' – Jason Donovan
'You'll Never Stop Me Loving You' – Sonia
'Do They Know It's Christmas?' – Band Aid 2
'Tears On My Pillow' – Kylie Minogue

— SORRY SEEMS TO BE THE HARDEST WORD —

Rock is a tolerant church, but some musicians still manage to go too far...

John Lennon
When he commented that The Beatles were 'bigger than Jesus' in 1966, Lennon's comments led to widespread burning of Beatles records.

David Bowie
At the height of Bowie's cocaine use in the mid-'70s, he gave a Nazi salute to waiting fans. The incident caused huge controversy and Bowie left the country altogether. He's been apologising for the gaffe ever since.

Eric Clapton
When the guitarist supported right-wing politician Enoch Powell in 1976, his drunken speech included references to Britain becoming a 'black colony' and suggested that it was time to 'get the foreigners out'. Rock Against Racism was formed as a direct result of his comments.

Kurt Cobain
The release of Nirvana's third album, *In Utero*, was bogged down in controversy thanks to the track 'Rape Me'. Intended as a pro-woman song, the song didn't come across that way and was castigated by womens' groups.

Janet Jackson
An 'accidental' flash of breast during the 2004 Superbowl ignited a storm of protest from family and Christian groups, briefly making Jackson the most hated woman in America.

Bono
The U2 frontman apologised to the whole of Ireland in 2004 when he was spotted flouting the country's ban on smoking in public places.

— SLIPKNOT STYLE —

Slipknot are notorious for their on-stage excesses: singer Corey Taylor enjoys sniffing dead crows and vomiting all over the place while the rest of the band attempt to put each other in casualty. As the *New Statesman* reported in 2002, at one US gig 'they took out a dead beaver, sucked its tail and head, squeezed its guts on to their faces and spent the next ten minutes vomiting all over the stage and on the audience.' Nice!

— STARS BEHIND BARS —
PART TWO

Tupac – The rapper spent six months in prison after being convicted of sexual assault in 1995, and he became the first artist to have a number 1 album while incarcerated.

Mick and Keith – Messrs Jagger and Richards served a few days at Her Majesty's Pleasure after a late-'60s police raid discovered some drugs in their possession. Keith Richards? On drugs? Surely not!

Johnny Cash – The Man In Black's prison concerts were legendary, but he also spent time as an inmate after he was caught picking flowers. No, really.

— POLITICAL SONGS – AND WHAT THEY'RE ABOUT —

Song	Artist	Political subject
'Pride (In The Name Of Love)'	U2	Civil rights
'Bad Day'	REM	US Republicanism and the media
'Straight To Hell'	The Clash	The plight of immigrants
'Shipbuilding'	Elvis Costello	The Falklands War
'Free Nelson Mandela'	Special AKA	Apartheid
'Do They Know It's Christmas'	Band Aid	Famine
'Free Satpal Ram'	Asian Dub Foundation	Miscarriage of justice
'Ghost Town'	The Specials	Urban decay
'God Save The Queen'	Sex Pistols	Anti-monarchism
'Biko'	Peter Gabriel	Apartheid
'Born In The USA'	Bruce Springsteen	Vietnam
'Chop Suey'	System Of A Down	Inner-city drugs
'Tramp The Dirt Down'	Elvis Costello	Wishing Margaret Thatcher dead
'The Lebanon'	Human League	Conflict in the Middle East
'Letter From America'	The Proclaimers	Depopulation via emigration
'Mercy Mercy Me (The Ecology)'	Marvin Gaye	Environmentalism

— RAPPERS' REAL NAMES —

50 Cent	Curtis Jackson
Bubba Sparxxx	Warren Mathis
Busta Rhymes	Trevor Smith
Chuck D	Carlton Ridenhour
DMX	Earl Simmons
Dr Dre	Andre Young
Eminem	Marshall Bruce Mathers III
Ginuwine	Elgin Lumpkin
Ice Cube	O'Shea Jackson
Ice-T	Tracey Morrow
Ja Rule	Jeffrey Atkins
Jay-Z	Shawn Carter
Kid Rock	Robert Ritchie
KRS One	Lawrence Krisna Parker
Lil Kim	Kimberly Jones
LL Cool J	James Smith
Ludacris	Christopher Bridges
MC Hammer	Stanley Burrell
Method Man	Clifford Smith
Ms Dynamite	Niomi McLean-Daley
Mos Def	Dante Terrell Smith
Nelly	Carnell Haynes Jr
Notorious BIG	Christopher Wallace
ODB	Russell Jones
Queen Latifah	Dana Owens
Redman	Reggie Noble
Roots Manuva	Rodney Smith
Sean Paul	Sean Paul Henriques
Snoop Doggy Dogg	Calvin Broadus
Suge Knight	Marion Hugh Knight Jr
Timbaland	Tim Mosely
Vanilla Ice	Robert Van Winkle
Xzibit	Alvin Joyner

— OUCH! —

The Who's Pete Townshend had a unique 'windmilling' way of playing guitar, but it wasn't exactly good for him: he'd regularly cut his hand to ribbons on the bridge of his guitar, and at one gig in the 1980s managed to impale his hand on his guitar's tremolo arm.

— SONGS THEY NEVER PLAY ON THE RADIO —

From moral panics in the '60s to political censorship during the Gulf War, radio stations have a long tradition of filtering the songs you can hear. Here are some of the most notable examples:

'A Day In The Life', The Beatles (1967): the BBC reckoned that the song included coded drug references. The line 'I'd love to turn you on' may have been a clue.

'Give Ireland Back To The Irish', Paul McCartney (1972): Macca's political protest was deemed too inflammatory in the wake of Bloody Sunday.

'God Save The Queen', The Sex Pistols (1977): incredibly, when the Pistols reached number 1 their anti-royal song was simply ignored by the charts.

'Relax', Frankie Goes To Hollywood (1984): Radio 1 DJ Mike Read spotted that the song was about sex and erupted in moral outrage. 'Relax' rocketed to number 1.

'We Call It Acieed', D-Mob (1988): an unfortunate victim of anti-drug hysteria, this rather bad record – which, ironically, had an anti-drug message – received almost no airplay.

Status Quo (1995): when Radio 1 banned Status Quo records on the grounds that they were a bit rubbish, the band sued. And lost.

'Smack My Bitch Up', The Prodigy (1997): radio programmers decided, reasonably enough, that songs about wife-beating weren't suitable for daytime radio.

'Millennium Prayer', Cliff Richard (1991): this Christmas number 1 received virtually no airplay, not because it was controversial but because it was truly, truly terrible: *The Lord's Prayer* to the tune of 'Auld Lang Syne'.

— PEOPLE MICK JAGGER HAS SHAGGED —

There are, of course, far too many notches on the rubber-lipped wrinkly's bedpost to be contained in these pages, but even a few of his high-profile conquests make for impressive reading. Mick's first girlfriend was Chrissie Shrimpton. Chrissie was the sister of a famous model, and Mick was obviously building up to the obsession with models he would later become legendary for. As well as his two model wives, Bianca Macias and Jerry Hall, he's bedded a string of models from around the world, including the British Nicole Kruk, Czech Jana Rajilch and Italian Carla Bruni. He shacked up with Marianne Faithfull for over three years in the late '60s, although not before she'd bedded several other Stones members.

The words 'have my baby' from the mouth of Marsha Hunt, star of the musical *Hair* were obviously too much for Jagger to resist and he gladly obliged, resulting in his first daughter. After a fling with groupie extraordinaire Pamela Des Barres, Mick shared his home with Catherine James and Janice Kenner (yes, at the same time) and bedded sex therapist Natasha Terry. It's not clear whether he was seeing her in a professional capacity. Although he was with Texan beauty Jerry Hall for many years, he didn't exactly calm down, and while having four children with her, he had a series of high-profile affairs. Their torrid marriage finally ended when Brazilian Luciana Morad gave birth to his seventh child. Guess what she does for a living? There's life in the old dog yet, then, and Sophie Dahl, Uma Thurman and Elle MacPherson are also rumoured to feature among recent conquests. Mr Jagger, we salute you.

— ABANDONED BAND NAMES —

Arabacus Pulp – **Pulp**
Bastard – **Motorhead**
Glass Onion – **Travis**
Johnny And The Self-Abusers – **Simple Minds**
Mark Skid And The Y-Fronts – **The Boomtown Rats**
Mookie Blaylock – **Pearl Jam**
On A Friday – **Radiohead**
Platinum Lotus Foundation – **Linkin Park**
Polar Bear – **Snow Patrol**
Rain – **Oasis**
Stiff Kittens – **Joy Division**
The Hype / Feedback – **U2**
The Patrol – **The Stone Roses**
The Swankers – **The Sex Pistols**

— FROM AOR TO MOR —

AOR (Adult Oriented Rock): Originally a descriptive term for intelligent rock music; now used primarily as an insult.

Blues Rock: Often a derogatory term, Blues Rock brings '40s blues up to date, largely by playing it more loudly

Country Rock: Rock music that borrows its melodic sense from country, such as The Eagles.

Emo: US rock genre largely populated by bookish boys singing about how unhappy they are.

Folk-Rock: Slightly more aggressive version of folk music incorporating electric instruments

Garage: Abrasive, amateurish and exciting rock music from bands who rehearse in their garages.

Goth: Doomy rock music for people who drink snakebite and dress in black, black and black.

Hardcore: Early '80s offshoot of punk that prized speed and aggression

Indie: Rock music from small, independent record labels. The term is almost meaningless today.

MOR (Middle Of the Road): Derogatory term for radio-friendly rock.

— THE WIT AND WISDOM OF THE GALLAGHERS — PART THREE

'If him and his gawky bird want to go banging on about the war they can do it at their own gigs. That lot are just a bunch of nobhead students. Chris Martin looks like a f***ing geography teacher. What's all that f***ing shit with writing messages about free trade on his hand when he's playing? If he wants to write things down I'll give him a f***ing pen and a pad of paper. Bunch of students!'

Liam on Coldplay, after a *Teenage Cancer Trust* fundraiser

— SCOT'S WA-HEY! —
CREDIBLE (AND CRINGEWORTHY) CALEDONIAN EXPORTS

Annie Lennox
Arab Strap
Aztec Camera
Belle and Sebastian
Beta Band
Big Country
Cocteau Twins
David Byrne
Deacon Blue
Del Amitri
Edwin Collins
Franz Ferdinand
Garbage*
Gerry Rafferty
Idlewild
Midge Ure
Mogwai
Mull Historical Society

Nazareth
Orange Juice
Primal Scream
Rod Stewart**
Runrig
Simple Minds
Snow Patrol***
Teenage Fanclub
Texas
The Associates
The Bay City Rollers
The Blue Nile
The Delgados
The Jesus And Mary Chain
The Proclaimers
The Sensational Alex Harvey Band
Travis
Wet Wet Wet

*   Singer Shirley Manson is from Edinburgh
**   Rod isn't actually Scottish: he was born in Highgate, London
***   Although from Northern Ireland, the band relocated to Scotland

— VOCAL PROBLEMS —

Vocal chord nodules – singers' nodes, polyps – are the curse of the vocalist. Elton John had his removed, which probably altered his voice, while Queen's Freddie Mercury simply ignored them.

More unusually, Joe Strummer contracted hepatitis when performing near the start of The Clash's career. An over-enthusiastic fan, engaging in the traditional punk show of affection of 'gobbing' on his heroes, rather uncharitably launched one straight down Strummer's throat, passing on hepatitis into the bargain.

But Maria Callas suffered most from throat problems, developing sermato-myositis, a muscle inflammation. She was prescribed prednisone – a steroid – which is thought to have affected her heart and eventually induced the attack that killed her.

— DRUMMER DEATHS —

'You can't dust for vomit' – *Spinal Tap*

It's well known that being a rock drummer is a risky profession, and here are a few who fell prey to the curse of percussion.

Keith Moon – The Who

The daddy of all drummers, Keith Moon was as mad as a hatter and pretty much invented rock 'n' roll – well, the kit-destroying, heavy drinking, throwing tellies out of window side of it anyway. Ironically, Keith died from an overdose of Heminevrin, which he was prescribed to help fight his alcoholism.

Karen Carpenter – The Carpenters

Singing drummer of brother and sister duo The Carpenters, Karen sold around 100 million copies of her touchy-feely pop before dying of a heart attack, brought on by anorexia, in 1983.

John 'Bonzo' Bonham – Led Zeppelin

There was a time when choking on one's own vomit was a must-have fashion accessory for rockstars with a deathwish, and Zep drummer Bonham was not to be left out, dying in his sleep after a huge drinks binge didn't agree with the drugs he was taking to keep him off heroin.

Pete De Freitas – Echo And The Bunnymen

Brought in to the scouse pseudo-goths when they got tired of their 'virtual drummer' Echo, De Freitas left the band in 1986 and died in a car crash in 1989.

Cozy Powell – Black Sabbath/Rainbow/Whitesnake

Not content with drumming for one legendary metal band, Powell played in three, as well as a number of other projects. He should have known better – he crashed his car outside Bristol and died. Ironic for a one-time racing driver.

— GG ALLIN —

The late GG Allin was notorious for his on-stage behaviour, which included hitting himself with bottles, urinating on himself, the band and the crowd, having sex on stage and inserting equipment where the sun doesn't shine.

— THE CRAZY WORLD OF FRANK ZAPPA —

Selected album and song titles by the late, great Frank Zappa:

Burnt Weeny Sandwich (1969)
Sheik Yerbouti (1979)
Ship Arriving Too Late To Save A Drowning Witch (1982)
Uncle Meat (1969)
Waka/Jawaka (1972)
Weasels Ripped My Flesh (1970)

'A Nun Suit Painted On Some Old Boxes'
'Alien Orifice'
'Baby, Take Your Teeth Out'
'Bwana Dik'
'Cletus Awreetus-Awrightus'
'Dental Hygiene Dilemma'
'Dew On The Newts We Got'
'Dickie's Such An Asshole'
'Dog Breath, In The Year Of The Plague'
'Don't You Ever Wash That Thing?'
'Electric Aunt Jemima'
'Food Gathering In Post-Industrial America, 1992'
'Frogs With Dirty Little Lips'
'Half A Dozen Provocative Squats'
'Ian Underwood Whips It Out'
'In-A-Gadda-Stravinsky'
'It Ain't Necessarily The Saint James Infirmary'
'Little Green Scratchy Sweaters & Corduroy Ponce'
'Lucy's Seduction Of A Bored Violinist & Postlude'
'Nasal Retentive Calliope Music'
'Penguin In Bondage'
'Poofter's Froth Wyoming Plans Ahead'
'Revenge Of The Knick Knack People'
'Sinister Footwear II'
'The Chrome Plated Megaphone Of Destiny'
'The Dangerous Kitchen'
'The Eric Dolphy Memorial Barbecue'
'Tryin' To Grow A Chin'
'Why Does It Hurt When I Pee?'
'Would You Like A Snack?'
'Zolar Czakl'

— FLEETWOOD MAC'S DOPPELGANGER PROBLEM —

Bands have legal problems all the time. But it's not often that one of the world's biggest bands discovers that they've been secretly replaced with fakes.

Fleetwood Mac were having problems with guitarists. Founder member Peter Green went a bit mad after being given LSD, and left the band. Guitarist Jeremy Spencer went out for groceries one day, joined a religious cult he bumped into in the street, and never came back. Guitarist Danny Kirwan broke down on stage and was fired. Replacement guitarist Bob Weston had an affair with – depending on which report you read – either Christine McVie (founder member John's wife), or Jenny Fleetwood (founder member Mick's wife), so was fired. At this point, in 1973, the band cancelled the rest of their US tour.

Their manager, Clifford Davis, was understandably exasperated. Here he was, manager of a band who had outsold The Beatles and Stones combined in 1969, and their instability was flushing money down the toilet. So he hit on an ingenious solution.

Various London musicians received mysterious telegrams instructing them to ring a phone number and not to tell a soul what was happening. On ringing the number, they were told to attend a top secret audition. Those who passed the audition were asked by Clifford Davis to join Fleetwood Mac. With this new band – containing not one real member of Fleetwood Mac – Davis was able to restart the previously cancelled US tour. They played Fleetwood Mac songs (pretty well, by all accounts); they had Fleetwood Mac's manager; they were called Fleetwood Mac. But not everyone was happy.

The American fans were furious, demanding to see the real group. Dave Wilkinson, keyboard player in the fake band, says that fans in New York were so angry, he thought he was going to be shot. Meanwhile, back in the UK, John and Mick, who had thought they were on a break, heard through the grapevine that their band were in fact touring the US. They entered into a year-long legal battle with Clifford Davis over the right to use their own name, eventually winning. The court took the view that you can't tell Mr Fleetwood and Mr MacVie that they can't use their own surnames.

The fake band changed their name to Stretch and had a hit single.

INSTRUMENTS PLAYED BY MIKE OLDFIED ON
— TUBULAR BELLS —

Grand piano
Piano
Honky-tonk piano
Farfisa organ
Hammond organ
Lowrey organ
Taped motor-drive amplifier organ chord
Bass guitar
Electric guitars
Speed guitar
Speed electric guitars
Guitars sounding like bagpipes
Fuzz guitars
Acoustic guitars
Spanish guitar
Mandolin-like guitar
Assorted percussion
Concert timpani
Glockenspiel
Flageolet
Tubular bells
Moribund chorus
Piltdown Man (this is the name given to the speeded-up
sound of Mike's drunken shouting)

Mandolin and violin aren't officially listed on the album, but experts with too much time on their hands reckon they're there as well.

Despite the many references to guitars, Mike actually just played the one electric guitar. The different descriptions refer to different electronic effects and recording techniques.

— PRETENTIOUS? MOI? —
PART TWO

'I smash guitars because I like them.'
Pete Townshend, The Who

'I have always had a repulsive need to be something more than human.'
David Bowie

— WAR! HUH! WHAT IS IT GOOD FOR? —

Famous anti-war songs and the conflicts that inspired them:

Song	Artist	War/Conflict
'Born In The USA'	Bruce Springsteen	Vietnam
'Brothers in Arms'	Dire Straits	All wars
'Enola Gay'	OMD	World War II (Hiroshima)
'For What It's Worth'	Buffalo Springfield	Vietnam
'Give Peace A Chance'	John Lennon	Vietnam
'Masters Of War'	Bob Dylan	All wars
'Shipbuilding'	Elvis Costello	The Falklands
'Sunday Bloody Sunday'	U2	The Troubles
'War'	Edwin Starr	All wars
'War Pigs'	Black Sabbath	Vietnam

— THE RELENTLESS RISE OF THE *TWEENAGER* —

Some of the world's worst records – Bob The Builder's 'Can We Fix It', 'Teletubbies Say Eh-Oh!', 'Make Way For Noddy' and the particularly hellish 'Orville's Song' – are sold in huge quantities thanks to the music industry's secret weapon: little children.

But it's not just kiddie-pop that's being bought by little tykes: it's all pop music. Teenagers are no longer the most important market for music; that honour goes to 'tweenagers', their pre-teen siblings aged between 8 and 12. While teenagers tend to buy rock, rap and R&B, tweenagers are responsible for the careers of acts such as Britney Spears, Christina Aguilera and almost every boy- and girl-band, not to mention the *Pop Idol* and *Fame Academy* winners. A recent report by research firm Datamonitor reports that the average UK tweenager receives £7.58 per week, with the spending power of children aged between 10 and 13 reaching a massive £1 billion per year.

— CLASSICALLY TRAINED ROCKERS —

Rick Wakeman: classically-trained pianist
Sky: led by classical guitarist John Williams
Tori Amos: classically-trained singer
Emerson, Lake and Palmer: guitarist Lake isn't classically-trained, but Palmer will apparently make up for it by insisting that he's a percussionist, not a drummer...

— A BRIEF HISTORY OF *ABBEY ROAD* STUDIOS —

Abbey Road Studio was opened in 1931 by The Gramophone Company, or EMI Records as we know them now. It owes much of its legendary status to its connections with The Beatles, but the list of artists that have used the studio is as long as an orang-utan's arm, and a host of movie scores have been recorded there as well. Originally designed for recording classical music, the first person to record there was Sir Edward Elgar, who recorded 'Land Of Hope And Glory' with the British National Symphony Orchestra, while violinist Yehudi Menuhin also used the studios in the '30s.

The Glen Miller Orchestra recorded their last album there, and this marked a branching out for Abbey Road. The first pop record to be recorded there was 'Move It' by Cliff Richard and his Drifters (later to become The Shadows). The floodgates were opened and a host of influential rock and pop artists started to use the studios, including Gene Pitney, Gerry And The Pacemakers and The Hollies. The recording of 'Love Me Do' in 1963 saw the start of The Beatles' seven-year love affair with Abbey Road and they were followed by the likes of Manfred Mann, Procol Harum, Eric Clapton and, ahem, Cilla Black. Pink Floyd dominated Abbey Road in the '70s, recording *Dark Side Of The Moon* and other albums there, and it has maintained its popularity to this day, being used by Kate Bush, Sting, Oasis and even The Spice Girls. The studios were also used for the scores to block-buster movies *Raiders Of The Lost Ark*, *Star Wars* (*Return Of The Jedi* and *The Phantom Menace*), *Braveheart* and *The Lord Of The Rings* trilogy.

You can find out more about Abbey Road at www.abbeyroad.co.uk.

— THE BIGGEST GIGS IN THE WORLD —

385,000	Blockbuster Rockfest, Texas, 1997
400,000	Woodstock (1969)
450,000	SARS Benefit, Toronto, 2003
500,000	Simon & Garfunkel, Central Park, 1981
600,000	Isle of Wight Festival, 1970
600,000	Summer Jam at Watkins Glen, New York, 1973
670,000	US Festival, California, 1983
750,000	Garth Brooks, Central Park, 1997
800,000	New York Philharmonic, Central Park, 1986
3.5 million	Rod Stewart, Rio De Janeiro, 1994

Source: Guinness World Records, askmen.com

— THE BIGGEST RECORD DEALS OF ALL TIME —

£30,000   The Sex Pistols

At the very beginning of the band's contract with EMI in 1977, their infamous appearance on the Bill Grundy show upset label bosses. EMI paid the band a reported £30,000 to leave the label.

£45 million ($80m)   REM

As one of the most successful bands in the world, REM had all the cards when they signed a new deal in 1996 and managed to squeeze £45 million from Warner Brothers. Their next album, *New Adventures In Hi-Fi*, sold poorly; drummer Bill Berry left the band the following year and the band's record sales have continued to slide.

£50 million ($90 million)   U2

U2's manager Paul McGuinness is one of the smartest men in the music business, and his financial acumen is legendary. Contract negotiations in 1993 persuaded the band's label to cough up $40m, and in 1998 he nabbed another $50m so the label could release the band's greatest hits. U2 is believed to have one of the highest royalty rates in music – as much as £3 per album – but as the band continues to sell millions of records, it's a rare example of a deal that's worked for artist and record label alike.

£71 million ($128m)   Mariah Carey

When Mariah Carey signed with Virgin/EMI in 2001, she was paid a reported $100m. Her next album was a flop, and her career showed few signs of recovery; just nine months after signing the deal, Carey was given her P45 and a further $28 million. She then signed with Island/Def Jam, who won't tell anyone how much the deal was worth.

£80 million   Robbie Williams

EMI again: this time, the label offered Robbie Williams a 'truly groundbreaking' contract in 2002. The six-album deal could be very lucrative for the label, as it gives them a cut not just of record sales but of tours, songwriting and merchandising income.

— NAMED AND SHAMED —

25 band names that should have stayed on the drawing board:

…And You Will Know Us By The Trail of Dead
Alien Ant Farm
An Emotional Fish
Anal C***
Butthole Surfers
Carter The Unstoppable Sex Machine
Dillinger Escape Plan
Dogs Die in Hot Cars
Dumpy's Rusty Nuts
Fast Food Rockers
Gay Dad
Har Mar Superstar
Hootie and the Blowfish
Insane Clown Posse
Limp Bizkit
Meat Beat Manifesto
Ned's Atomic Dustbin
Puddle of Mudd
Sixpence None the Richer
Squirrel Nut Zippers
Terminal Cheesecake
The 80s Matchbox B-Line Disaster
The Yeastie Girls
Throbbing Gristle
Toad The Wet Sprocket

— TAT'S ENTERTAINMENT: TATTOOS OF THE STARS — PART THREE

Fatboy Slim: Smiley face with cross-bones on his arm

Dave Grohl (Foo Fighters): Chain on upper right arm, FF on back of neck

Geri Halliwell: Black panther on lower back, star on upper back

Kid Rock: Detroit Tigers' D on right arm, PAUL on left bicep, large back piece with the words AMERICAN BAD ASS and a bald eagle

— A SPINAL TAP DISCOGRAPHY —

1967	*Spinal Tap Sings '(Listen To The) Flower People' And Other Songs*
1968	*We Are All Flower People*
1969	*Silent But Deadly* (Live Album)
1970	*Brainhammer*
1971	*Nerve Damage*
1972	*Blood To Let*
1974	*Intravenus De Milo*
1975	*The Sun Never Sweats*
1975	*Jap Habit* (Triple Live Album)
1976	*Bent For The Rent*
1977	*Tap Dancing*
1980	*Shark Sandwich*
1982	*Smell The Glove*
1983	*Heavy Metal Memories*
1984	*Original Soundtrack from This Is Spinal Tap*
1984	'Christmas With The Devil'
1992	*Break Like The Wind*
1992	'Bitch School'
1992	'The Majesty Of Rock' (with roast beef scratch 'n' sniff sticker)

Unreleased albums include *Flak Packet*, *Here's More Tap*, and *Lusty Lorry*.

— COLLECTABLE RECORDS —
(SOME RECENT AUCTION PRICES)

The Beatles – *Yesterday And Today* LP (sealed, butcher sleeve):
$38,500 (1999)
Billy Ward & His Dominoes – 10-inch LP:
$24,200 (1999)
Jean-Michel Jarre – *Musique Pour Supermarché* master plates
(he'd destroyed all other copies):
FF69,000, approximately $10,000 (2003)
Frank Wilson's 'Do I Love You' 45
£15,000 (1999)
The Beatles – *Please Please Me* (signed)
£5,700 (2004)

— WELL-QUALIFIED ROCK STARS –

DK Smythe (Rezillos):	Has a doctorate in geophysics
Tony James (Generation X & Sigue Sigue Sputnik):	Has a degree in maths
Brian May:	Boasts a degree in astronomy
Iron and Wine:	Singer Sam Beam is a professor of film and cinematography
Althea & Donna:	Donna of the reggae one-hit wonders is now a qualified New York council administrator
Kathleen Battle:	As well as Emmys, the jazz singer's fireplace groans under the weight of bachelor's and master's degrees
Bad Religion:	The American punkers have no fewer than two doctorates to their name
The Clash:	Drummer Terry Chimes is now a qualified chiropractor
Matt Jenson:	The Berklee lecturer, assistant professor and pianist developed a studies class around Bob Marley's work
Radiohead:	All have degrees apart from youngster Jonny
Bruce Dickinson (Iron Maiden):	Has a pilot's license
Dave Greenfield (Stranglers):	Has a pilot's license

— NAME THAT TUNE —

Ten songs where the name of the song doesn't appear in the lyrics:

Blur – 'Song 2'
New Order – 'Blue Monday'
The Beatles – 'Ballad Of John And Yoko'
The Rolling Stones – 'Sympathy For The Devil'
The Who – 'Baba O'Riley'
U2 – '40'
Smiths – 'Paint A Vulgar Picture'
REM – 'So. Central Rain'
Radiohead – 'Lucky'
Red Hot Chili Peppers – 'The Greeting Song'

— THE TRUCK DRIVER'S GEAR CHANGE —

The Truck Driver's Gear Change is a cheap-and-nasty songwriting technique – often used towards the end of a song, when the ideas have run out and a new lease of life is required – which involves *modulating* suddenly 'up a key'. The effect evokes the sensation of a truck being forced into a new gear with minimal clutch control.

The godfather of the gear change (which in the majority of cases consists of an upwards movement by a semitone) is generally recognised to be Barry Manilow, most of whose songs seem to be marred by unnecessary key shifts. However, the uncharismatic boy band Westlife have given him a good run for his money, to the point of covering one of his more offensive gear changes in the form of 'Mandy'. For sheer modulation overload, a trawl through the Eurovision Song Contest entries in any given year usually challenges even the most hardened masochist. (See 'Eurovision Winners' above, for examples.)

Here are five particularly gruesome truck driver's gear changes:

'Downtown' – Petula Clark
A sixties classic, spoiled only by an unexpected key change which takes the song in an abruptly uptown direction.

'I Just Called To Say I Love You' – Stevie Wonder
This double gear change, which helps to stretch an already dubious song out for much too long, was definitely not Stevie Wonder's finest hour.

'Money, Money, Money' – ABBA
Unprovoked and unannounced, Benny and Björn's sudden key shift is quite disturbing.

'Man In The Mirror' – Michael Jackson
This song features a distressing self-consciousness in its lyrics, when after a short stop, the word 'change!' is shouted to herald the new key.

'Livin' On A Prayer' – Bon Jovi
Leaping upwards with a stratospheric lack of tact was evidently not sufficient for the New Jersey rockers, who hammer the point home by missing out the fourth beat in the bar at the moment of modulation.

For more on gear changes, visit www.gearchange.org

— CONCEPT ALBUMS —

While an album is a mere collection of songs, a concept album is supposed to have a grand unifying theme.

1967's *Sergeant Pepper's Lonely Hearts Club Band* is usually regarded as the first attempt at a concept album, although, as The Beatles themselves readily admitted, the concept never made it much further than the first two songs and the artwork.

In the same year, The Pretty Things released *SF Sorrow*, which tells a character's life story, and The Moody Blues released *Days Of Future Passed*, about a day in the life of an ordinary man. In 1968, The Who released *Tommy*, the story of a boy who is psychologically disturbed by witnessing his mother and her lover murder his father, becomes obsessed with pinball, and goes on to start his own religion.

Released in 1963, The Beach Boys' *Little Deuce Coupe* predates all of these, but opinion differs as to whether it qualifies as a concept album. If it does, its concept is pretty simple: every song is about cars.

Here are some more:

The War Of The Worlds – Jeff Wayne
The Rise And Fall Of Ziggy Stardust And The Spiders From Mars – David Bowie
We're Only In It For The Money – Frank Zappa & The Mothers Of Invention
Lola Vs. Powerman – The Kinks
Pictures At An Exhibition – Emerson, Lake & Palmer
The Lamb Lies Down On Broadway – Genesis
Captain Fantastic And The Brown Dirt Cowboy – Elton John
Alice Cooper Goes To Hell – Alice Cooper
Misplaced Childhood – Marillion
Seventh Son Of A Seventh Son – Iron Maiden
The Songs Of Distant Earth – Mike Oldfield
RZA As Bobby Digital In Stereo – RZA
Wormwood: Curious Stories From The Bible – The Residents
N.E.W.S. – Prince
American Idiot – Green Day
The Raven – Lou Reed
A Grand Don't Come For Free – The Streets

STARS WHO HAVE SUNG THE AMERICAN NATIONAL
— ANTHEM AT THE SUPER BOWL —

Super Bowl XVI:	Diana Ross
Super Bowl XVIII:	Barry Manilow
Super Bowl XXI:	Neil Diamond
Super Bowl XXII:	Herb Alpert
Super Bowl XXIII:	Billy Joel
Super Bowl XXIV:	Aaron Neville
Super Bowl XXV:	Whitney Houston
Super Bowl XXVI:	Harry Connick Jr.
Super Bowl XXVII:	Garth Brooks
Super Bowl XXVIII:	Natalie Cole
Super Bowl XXX:	Vanessa Williams
Super Bowl XXXI:	Luther Vandross
Super Bowl XXXII:	Jewel
Super Bowl XXXIII:	Cher
Super Bowl XXXIV:	Faith Hill
Super Bowl XXXV:	Backstreet Boys
Super Bowl XXXVI:	Mariah Carey

— PRODUCT PLACEMENT —
Ten songs featured in ads:

Artist	Product	Song
The Ramones	Budweiser Light	'Blitzkrieg Bop'
The Pretenders	Rover cars	'Brass In Pocket'
The Clash	Levi's	'Should I Stay Or Should I Go'
Fatboy Slim	Adidas	'Right Here, Right Now'
Grover Washington	Carling lager	'Just The Two Of Us'
Babylon Zoo	Levi's	'Spaceman'
The Fall	Vauxhall Corsa	'Touch Sensitive'
Velvet Underground	Dunlop Tyres	'Venus In Furs'
The Buzzcocks	Arthur's cat food	'What Do I Get'
Faithless	Vodafone	'The Garden'

— UNCHAINED MELODY —

Alex North's 'Unchained Melody' is one of the world's most popular songs, and it's been covered by artist after artist since it entered the charts in 1955: according to the *All Music Guide*, it has turned up on 801 different records including instrumental albums, live albums and easy listening collections.

— TEN SONGS COVERED BY REM —

- 'Academy Flight Song' – Mission Of Burma

- 'Arms Of Love' – Robyn Hitchcock

- 'Born To Run' – Bruce Springsteen

- 'Dark Globe' – Syd Barrett

- 'Does Your Mother Know?' – Abba

- 'Holiday In Cambodia' – Dead Kennedys

- 'Hootenanny' – Replacements

- 'Love Is All Around' – The Troggs

- 'Sex Bomb' – Flipper

- 'Strange' – Wire

— MOST CONSECUTIVE NUMBER 1 SINGLES —

The Beatles (surprise, surprise) set the record for consecutive number 1s. 'A Hard Day's Night' started the run when it topped the charts in July 1964, and was followed by 'I Feel Fine', 'Ticket To Ride', 'Help', 'Day Tripper' / 'We Can Work It Out', 'Paperback Writer' and finally 'Yellow Submarine' / 'Eleanor Rigby' in August 1966. 'Penny Lane' / 'Strawberry Fields Forever' ended the amazing run when it could only manage the pitiful position of number 2. Six of the band's next seven singles also reached number 1; an astonishing reminder of just how serious Beatlemania was.

The record was equalled by Irish boy band Westlife in 2000. Much-helped by the pop media machine, their debut single 'Swear It Again' went to number 1 in May 1999 and their run of seven, including 'Against All Odds' with Mariah Carey finally ended when 'What Makes A Man' peaked at number 2. The group went on another run of three consecutive number 1s in 2001/2002.

— TAKE THAT VS THE SPICE GIRLS —

First Take That and then The Spice Girls were rolled off the production line to dominate the charts in the 1990s but members of both groups have had mixed fortunes since breaking out on their own. Robbie Williams managed to shake off the boy band image to become a huge solo star, and Ginger Spice Geri Halliwell kept her solo career alive for a while amid publicity stunts and er, going out with Chris Evans. Many others did not fare so well.

TAKE THAT

Member	Number 1s	Top Ten	Top Forty
Robbie Williams	5	13	1
Gary Barlow	2	1	3
Mark Owen	0	3	3
Jason Orange	0	0	0
Howard Donald	0	0	0

THE SPICE GIRLS

Member	Number 1s	Top Ten	Top Forty
Geri Halliwell	4	3	0
Mel C	2	4	3
Mel B	1	2	2
Emma Bunton	1	1	2
Victoria Beckham	0	4	0

— SCANDINAVIAN DEATH METAL BANDS —

Bathory (Sweden)
Bloodbath (Sweden)
Dark Tranquility (Sweden)
Entomed (Sweden)
Regurgitate (Sweden)
Abominat (Norway)
Panzerchrist (Denmark)
Gehenna (Norway)
Burzum (Norway)
Dissection (Sweden)
Emperor (Norway)*
Mayhem (Norway)**

Their drummer is in prison for knifing a homosexual to death
**Their lead singer, ironically titled Dead, committed suicide in 1991.
Founder Euronymous was killed by a member of Burzum two years
later. Then, the bassist killed the guitarist for 'shaming' the scene. His
crime? Wearing a white sweater. We don't make this up.*

— BOX OFFICE PULLING POWER —

Do rock stars pull in punters to the films in which they star? Here are the gross USA box office figures for various stars' films:

Austin Powers In Goldmember (Beyoncé)	$213,079,163
The Bodyguard (Whitney Houston)	$121,945,720
8 Mile (Eminem)	$116,724,075
Three Kings (Mark Wahlberg)	$60,652,036
Mask (Cher)	$42,400,000
Dune (Sting)	$27,400,000
The Player (Lyle Lovett)	$21,706,100
Freejack (Mick Jagger)	$17,129,000
Gigli (Jennifer Lopez)	$6,068,735
Dancer In The Dark (Bjork)	$4,157,491
The Krays (Martin Kemp)	$2,060,847
Swept Away (Madonna)	$598,645
Buster (Phil Collins)	$540,000
Million Dollar Hotel (Bono)	$52,526

Figures accurate as at 1 August 2004

— FAMOUS FRIENDS —

Thanks to the wonders of sampling and mash-ups, the charts are full of unlikely collaborations; however, there's a long tradition of musicians appearing on their famous friends' records – not as samples, but in the flesh.

Here are ten of the best:

Artist	Famous Friend	Song
Mott The Hoople	David Bowie	'All The Young Dudes'
Eminem	Dido	'Stan'
Michael Jackson	Eddie Van Halen	'Thriller'
George Harrison	Eric Clapton	'While My Guitar Gently Weeps'
The Cult	Iggy Pop	'Fire Woman'
U2	Johnny Cash	'The Wanderer'
Kristin Hersh	Michael Stipe	'Your Ghost'
Michael Jackson	Slash	'Black Or White'
PJ Harvey	Thom Yorke	'This Mess We're In'
Robbie Robertson	U2	'Sweet Fire Of Love'

— THE BEST LIVE VENUES IN BRITAIN —

Everybody has their own favourite venue, whether it's a sweat pit or a flash concert hall, but we've taken the facts, the figures, the awards and the reputations into account to come up with the five best in the country.

Brixton Academy, London

This legendary hall is constantly receiving awards. In 2004 alone, it was named Live Venue Of The Year in the *Time Out* Awards, Best Live Venue in the *NME* Awards and the production industry's Favourite Venue. It's played host to pretty much every band in the business from The Strokes to Status Quo and The Beach Boys (at the same time!).

- *Best Feature:* Incredible atmosphere
- *Interesting Fact:* Two tickets for Madonna's November 2002 gig here were auctioned on E-Bay for a staggering £2,204!

Barrowland, Glasgow

Like Brixton Academy, 'The Barras' isn't the biggest venue, but it's one of the best, noted for its riotous atmosphere. In a 2003 Radio 1 poll of over 60 rock bands, this was named as the best venue.

- *Best Feature:* Springy floor
- *Interesting Fact:* Once a popular ballroom.

Manchester Apollo

A former cinema and variety hall, Manchester Apollo is another place anyone who's anyone has played, from The Beatles to the Manics. Its removable seats allow for a larger capacity for standing gigs.

- *Best Feature:* Ice cream kiosk
- *Interesting Fact:* Opened in the '30s by movie star Margaret Lockwood.

Nottingham Rock City

With an exterior more like a warehouse than an international venue, the cavernous Rock City houses several rooms that host gigs and club nights.

- *Best Feature:* The famous sticky floors
- *Interesting Fact:* *Kerrang* 'Club Of The Year' every year from 1986–2004 and still holding the title.

King Tut's Wah Wah Hut, Glasgow

Small and sweaty with a capacity of just 300, King Tut's consistently wins awards as Britain's best small venue – it's the perfect place to get up close and personal with rock's finest.

- *Best Feature:* Getting close to the stage
- *Interesting Fact:* Alan McGee discovered Oasis here

— TOP TEN THIRD DIVISION PUNK BANDS —

999
UK Subs
Slaughter and the Dogs
Lurkers
Zones
Chelsea
Art Attacks
Drones
Eater
Crisis

— DOWNLOADING MUSIC: FOR AND AGAINST —

Artist	For/Against	Quote
Metallica	Against	'This is about piracy.'
Public Enemy	For	'Those scare tactics are pure Gestapo.'
Creed	Against	'Napster is robbing me blind.'
Grateful Dead	For	'They're protecting an archaic industry.'
Disturbed	For	'They have to learn how to effectively use the internet.'
Steve Miller	Against	'My record royalties have dropped 80% since 1999...'
Britney Spears	Against	'It's stealing.'
Dixie Chicks	Against	'It may seem innocent...'
Janis Ian	For	'If a music industry executive claims I should agree with their agenda because it will make me more money, I put my hand on my wallet and check it after they leave, just to make sure nothing is missing.'

— THE WIT AND WISDOM OF THE GALLAGHERS —
PART FOUR

'If a guy suddenly appears before me with a big beard and locks and all that caper and performed some f***ing miracle, and then said to me "Liam, I am God", I'd say "Fair enough, it's a fair cop. I didn't believe in you but fair play, you've got me". But until that day comes he can f*** right off.'
Liam on God

— I WRITE THE SONGS —

The backroom boys (and girls) behind the biggest hits...

Alison Clarkson: In her former career as songstress Betty Boo, Clarkson performed bubblegum pop; these days, she writes hits for bands such as Hear'Say, Girls Aloud and, er, The Tweenies.

Andy McClusky: The former OMD singer formed – and wrote the songs for – girl band Atomic Kitten, whose success make his former band's sales look titchy.

Brian Higgins: The keyboardist in defunct dance band Motiv8 may not be a household name, but the artists who perform his songs are: Cher, Sugababes, Girls Aloud and even New Order.

Cathy Dennis: Another former pop performer, Dennis wrote Britney Spears' 'Toxic', Kylie's 'Can't Get You Out Of My Head' and many, many more.

Gary Clark: As singer with Danny Wilson, Clark failed to set the world on fire; however, he now works as a songwriter for hire with artists such as Natalie Imbruglia and Mel C.

Linda Perry: Her band – 4 Non Blondes – were awful, but Perry is the songwriter of choice for today's alternative female rockers, bestowing her talents on artists including Pink, Christina Aguilera, Courtney Love and Gwen Stefani.

Max Martin: The former singer of Swedish heavy metal band It's Alive dominates pop music: he wrote 'Baby One More Time' for Britney, and has written global smash hits for Celine Dion and the Backstreet Boys.

Rob Davis: Davis was once the guitarist in '70s glam rock band Mud; today, he's a songwriter for acts such as Kylie, Sonique, Samantha Mumba and Shaznay Lewis.

— IT'S NOT BIG, AND IT'S NOT CLEVER —

10 songs that feature a *lot* of swearing:

Ian Dury – 'Plaistow Patricia'
Opening line: 'Assholes, b***tards, f***ing c***s and pricks'
Sex Pistols – 'Friggin' In The Riggin''
See also their sensitive ballad, 'Bodies'
John Cooper Clarke – 'Chickentown'
This really doesn't let up!
Chaotic Dischord – 'F*** Religion, F*** Politics, F*** The Lot Of You'
Does what it says on the tin...
Dead Kennedys – 'Too Drunk To F***'
Details the effects of inebriation on romantic conquests
Super Furry Animals – 'The Man Don't Give A F***'
Featuring no less than 53 uses of the 'f' word
Fatboy Slim – 'F***ing In Heaven'
An even more impressive 108...
Derek And Clive – 'Winkie Wanky Woo'
The inimitable Pete 'n' Dud combo
NWA – F*** Tha Police
Ice Cube was no fan of the boys in blue
The Yeastie Girls – You Suck
Feminist dinner party-spoiler addresses oral equality issues

— THIRTEEN SONGS ABOUT THATCHERISM —

'Thatcher Years' – New Model Army
'Tramp The Dirt Down' – Elvis Costello
'Ironmasters' – Men They Couldn't Hang
'Thatcherites' – Billy Bragg
'Stand Down Margaret' – The Beat
'Margaret On The Guillotine' – The Smiths
'Tea With Pinochet' – Christy Moore
'Two Million Voices' – Angelic Upstarts
'I'm In Love With Margaret Thatcher' – Notsensibles
'Kick Out The Tories' – Newtown Neurotics
'Sheep Farming In The Falklands' – Crass
'Celebrate (The Day After You)' – Blow Monkeys
'The Day That Thatcher Dies' – Hefner

— ROCK STARS' RELIGIONS —

Adam Yauch (Beastie Boys)	Buddhism
Bob Dylan	Judaism and then born-again Christianity
Bob Marley	Rastafarian
Bono	Former member of evangelical Christian organisation*
Cat Stevens	Islam
Freddie Mercury	Zoroastrian
George Harrison	Hare Krishna
Ice Cube	Nation of Islam
Madonna	Kaballah Buddhism
Marilyn Manson	Satanism**
Michael Jackson	Nation of Islam***
The Osmonds	Mormons
Mick Jagger	Kaballah Buddhism
Slash	Judaism
Sting	Buddhism

* *Along with The Edge and Larry Mullen Jr., Bono was a member of Christian organisation Shalom*
** *So he says, although Manson tends to tell porkies to wind up the moral majority*
*** *Jackson's 2004 alliance with the NoI was shortlived and dismissed by many as a publicity stunt*

FIVE THINGS YOU DIDN'T — KNOW ABOUT THE BEATLES—

1. The working title for 'Yesterday' was 'Scrambled Eggs'.
2. In his Beatles days, Paul McCartney had three cats named Jesus, Mary and Joseph.
3. Without his glasses, John Lennon was legally blind.
4. Contrary to popular belief, The Beatles' first American TV appearance was on the *Jack Paar Show*, not the *Ed Sullivan Show*.
5. The band's first album *Please Please Me* was recorded in a single day.

— THE FOOTBALL/ROCK CROSSOVER—

Being spotted at a footy game has become vital to the maintenance of a pop star's street cred, and growing numbers of them have popped up at stadia around the country. Unsurprisingly, **Chelsea**'s Stamford Bridge plays host to the biggest number of West End celebs. As well as a host of TV stars, Blur's Damon Albarn, superstar DJ Paul Oakenfold and Madness members Suggs and Woody can be found there. London rivals **Arsenal** and **Tottenham Hotspur** also boast a healthy roster of rock and pop hangers-on. **Arsenal** can claim Spandau Ballet's Kemp brothers, songstress Dido, DJ Pete Tong and even former S-Clubber Rachel Stevens among their number, while husky '80s crooner Paul Young lays his hat at **Spurs'** White Hart Lane, along with Phil Collins, Emma 'Baby Spice' Bunton, Status Quo and the godlike Chas 'n' Dave.

Moving north, Sir Paul McCartney claims to be an **Everton** fan, while his old mucker Cilla Black is on the other side of the Scouse divide, following **Liverpool**, as do Chris De Burgh, Mark Owen and Mel C. In Manchester, Oasis siblings Noel and Liam Gallagher's allegiance to **Manchester City** is well-documented, though the club probably don't boast as much about *Coronation Street* star and brief pop star Adam Rickett. Rivals **Manchester United** do a little better, counting indie legends Ian Brown (The Stone Roses) and Richard Ashcroft (The Verve) among their fan base, although they also have to put up with Simply Red's Mick Hucknall.

In Scotland, **Celtic** top the charts with Rod Stewart, Simple Minds, Garbage's Shirley Manson, Del Amitri and Westlife proclaiming their support. Other well-known footy fans include Stereophonics' Kelly Jones (**Leeds United**), Chris Rea (**Middlesbrough**), Robbie Williams (**Port Vale**), Craig David (**Southampton**) and Elton John (**Watford**).

— UK MUSIC MAGS: PAST AND PRESENT —

Bang!	Short-lived *Q* rival. Folded in 2003
College Music Journal (CMJ)	UK version of popular US student title
Careless Talk Costs Lives	Cult magazine launched by former *Melody Maker* writers
Drowned In Sound	Online only (*www.drownedinsound.com*)
Is This Music?	Scotland only magazine about independent and unsigned music
Kerrang!	Heavy metal magazine. Now has its own TV station
Melody Maker	Merged with *NME* in 2000
Metal Hammer	Rival to *Kerrang!*
Mojo	*Q* for old people. Very much alive and kicking
NME	The best-known – and now the only – UK music weekly
Plan B	Sequel to *Careless Talk Costs Lives*
Q	Was the UK's favourite rock monthly, but sales are slipping
Record Mirror	*NME* and *Melody Maker* rival. Folded in 1991
Rock Sound	Small, lower-budget rival to *Q*
Select	Britpop-loving *Q* rival. Folded in 2000
Smash Hits	Long-running music mag for younger readers
Sounds	'70s rival to *NME* and *Melody Maker*. Folded in 1992
The Fly	Free music magazine distributed at Barfly venues
The Wire	For fans of 'intelligent' music
Uncut	Monthly version of *NME* for older readers
Word	New-ish music monthly from the people who launched *Q*
X-Ray	Ill-fated magazine from XFM. Folded in early 2004

— SAFETY IN NUMBERS —

The bands with the largest number of personnel:

Earth Wind and Fire
They came mob-handed...
The Polyphonic Spree
You've brought your own CHOIR?
The Golden Palominos
43-ish and counting...
UK Subs
Well, in terms of personnel passing through,
over 120 at the last count
Test Department
Augmented the core group with full-blown orchestras
Wu-Tang Clan
Every one of 'em with a solo deal too...
So Solid Crew
Nobody knows for sure exactly how many members there are
Goldie Lookin Chain
Newport hip-hoppers with numerous personnel
Banda Del Recoda
19-odd strong Mexican institution

— WORDS OF WARNING —

'Never Die Young'	James Taylor
'Don't Be Cruel'	Elvis Presley
'World Shut Your Mouth'	Julian Cope
'Don't Eat The Yellow Snow'	Frank Zappa & The Mothers Of Invention
'Don't Look Back In Anger'	Oasis
'Never Do Anything'	Barenaked Ladies
'Don't Fight It, Feel It'	Primal Scream
'Don't Let Me Down'	The Beatles
'Stop Whispering'	Radiohead
'Never Believe'	Ministry
'Don't Let Us Get Sick'	Warren Zevon
'Don't Believe The Hype'	Public Enemy
'Don't Stop Me Now'	Queen

— YOUR TIME WILL COME —

Some artists had a long wait before they got their turn in the spotlight...

The Chi-Lites: Typical of many hard working vocal R&B groups, they had been recording for a decade before they finally had a hit in the late '60s.

David Gray: First signed in 1992, didn't break through until *White Ladder* in 1998.

Pulp: Formed when Jarvis Cocker was 15 in 1978, their first major success came in 1994 with *His 'n' Hers*.

The Stranglers: They'd been knocking around for at least five years in one form or another before punk happened.

Alvin Stardust: Had a few hits in the early '60s as Shane Fenton before adopting his alter ego to ride the glam bandwagon in 1973.

The Wurzels: They'd been around and about, including having a very minor hit single, since the mid-'60s, before they really 'hit the hay' in 1977 with 'Brand New Combine Harvester'.

Ian Dury: Before *New Boots And Panties* hit in 1978, ex-art school teacher Dury had been a regular on the pub rock scene since 1970.

Eva Cassidy: Only became a global star in 1998, sadly, two years after her death.

— BANDS THAT SING IN WELSH —

- Gorky's Zygotic Mynci
- Super Furry Animals
- Datblygu
- Llwybr Llaethog
- Ellifant
- Anhrefn
- Mogwai
- Big Leaves

— CLASSIC PEEL SESSIONS —

Tim Buckley (1968)
A majestic suite of five songs – its eventual release the singular purpose
behind Peel's 'Strange Fruit' record label
Ivor Cutler (1969)
Perennial Peel fave, including 'In My Room Sits A Box'
Fleetwood Mac (1970)
Recorded at the Paris Cinema, part of this was used on *Merely A
Portmanteau*
T Rex (1970)
Recorded when the band were still just a duo and featuring an early
version of 'Ride A White Swan'
The Damned (1977)
They were first to do just about everything, punk-wise
Siouxsie And The Banshees
Recorded when there were rumours that the Banshees would
sign to the BBC
Joy Division (1979)
Their Peel bow, featuring both 'She's Lost Control' and 'Transmission'
Misty In Roots (1979)
As well as supporting punk and post-punk, Peel was the place to catch
both Jamaican and Brit reggae
Birthday Party (1980)
Introducing Mr Nicholas Cave...
House Of Love (1988)
The great lost indie band of the late '80s
The Fall (1978–2003)
Twenty-three sessions and counting!
Cinerama (January 2002)
David Gedge leaves behind longstanding Peel faves Wedding Present but
still gets Uncle Peel's nod

— A DOMESTIC DISPUTE IN EIGHT SONGS—

'Come Talk To Me'	Peter Gabriel
'I Don't Want To Talk About It'	Rod Stewart
'Talk Talk'	Talk Talk
'Don't Speak'	No Doubt
'We Gotta Talk'	Jennifer Lopez
'Silence Is Golden'	Frankie Valli
'Gimme Some Truth'	John Lennon
'Shaddap Your Face'	Joe Dolce

— LOUIE, LOUIE —

'Louie, Louie' is one of the most famous rock songs of all time, and it ignited a moral panic in 1963 when The Kingsmen's version of the song was believed to be obscene. The song's reputation spread so quickly that the FBI become involved, carrying out an investigation that lasted almost three years. However, the 'dirty' version of the song didn't exist; as the urban legends site *snopes.com* points out, 'lead singer Jack Ely had strained his voice participating in a marathon 90-minute jam the night before the session; Ely was singing with braces on his teeth; the boom microphone in the studio was fixed way too high for Ely, who had to stand on tiptoe and sing into the mike; what the band thought was a rehearsal run-through turned out to be the one and only take of the song.'

Here is an excerpt of the real – and distinctly clean – lyrics:

Louie, Louie,
Me gotta go.
Louie, Louie,
Me gotta go.

A fine little girl, she wait for me;
Me catch a ship across the sea.
I sailed the ship all alone;
I never think I'll make it home.

— WHERE ARE THEY NOW? —

Terry Chimes	Drummer, The Clash	Chiropractor
Jim Martin	Guitarist, Faith No More	Pumpkin Farmer
Neal Smith	Drummer, Alice Cooper	Estate Agent
Stan Cullimore	Bassist, The Housemartins	Children's author
Roy Boulter	Drummer, The Farm	TV scriptwriter
Bill Berry	Drummer, REM	Farmer
Bragi Olafsson	Bassist, Sugarcubes	Copywriter
Francis Dunnery	Singer, It Bites	Astrologist
Donna Read	Singer, Anthea & Donna	Council administrator
Plastic Bertrand	French punk rocker	TV Director

— MIKE OLDFIELD'S STUDIO TECHNIQUES —

While making *Tubular Bells*, Mike Oldfield created some very weird noises, all before the days of synths. For a start, he recorded some of the guitar parts while running the tape at half-speed, resulting in high-pitched, double-speed bleepy guitar noises. Next, he wanted to make a guitar sound like bagpipes. According to *www.mikeoldfield.org*, Mike did this using the slightly mysterious Glorfindel box, an effects unit encased in a wooden box, which had been given to one of Mike's friends at a party by its creator, a stoned hippy. The Glorfindel was extremely unreliable, rarely giving the same result twice. According to ear-witness reports, the sounds it produced were only occasionally any good. On this occasion, Mike plugged the guitar into the Glorfindel box and got a heavily compressed and smoothly distorted guitar sound. He recorded lots of tracks of this noise, some at half-speed, ending up with a sound like bagpipes.

Mike felt one of the *Tubular Bells'* sections needed an extra sound, but couldn't work out what. While drunk, he decided to scream at the microphone while the tape was running slowly. This is the famous 'Piltdown Man' effect.

— SUICIDE IS PAINLESS —

Nick Drake: Overdosed on anti-depressants in 1974, although there is still controversy over whether his death was deliberate.

Kurt Cobain: Turned a shotgun on himself in 1994. Inevitably, conspiracy theories suggest that he was murdered.

Ian Curtis: The troubled Joy Division frontman hung himself in 1980, just before the band embarked on their debut US tour.

Darby Crash: Singer with influential punk band The Germs, Crash died of a deliberate heroin overdose in 1980.

Michael Hutchence: Hutchence was found to have hung himself with a leather belt in 1997, possibly in a sex game that went horribly wrong.

Elliott Smith: The critically acclaimed singer-songwriter killed himself with a single stab wound in October 2003.

Richie Edwards: The Manic Street Preachers guitarist disappeared in 1995, and is generally believed to have committed suicide.

— INSPIRED BY THE MOVIES —

Band	Inspired by
10,000 Maniacs	A B-movie called *2,000 Maniacs*
3 Colours Red	Krzysztof Kieslowski's *Three Colours Red*
Babes In Toyland	A 1934 Laurel & Hardy film
Bad Company	Lifted from a film poster
Black Rebel Motorcycle Club	From *The Wild One*, starring Marlon Brando
Black Sabbath	From the '60s Boris Karloff horror film of the same name
BMX Bandits	'80s movie starring Nicole Kidman
Duran Duran	A villain in *Barbarella* (1968)
Faster Pussycat	Russ Meyer's *Faster Pussycat! Kill! Kill!*
Heaven 17	A band mentioned in *Clockwork Orange*
Ministry	*Ministry Of Fear*, Fritz Lang (1946)
Mogwai	The cute one in *Gremlins*
Moloko	The milk drink in *Clockwork Orange*
Mudhoney	From another Russ Meyer film
My Bloody Valentine	A 1981 horror film
Pussy Galore	One of the characters in *Goldfinger*
T'Pau	One of the Vulcans in *Star Trek*
Texas	*Paris, Texas* by Wim Wenders
Travis	A character in *Paris, Texas*
They Might Be Giants	An early '70s movie title

— FORMER JOBS OF THE STARS —

Billy Bragg	Goatherd
Eric Clapton	Postman
Elvis Costello	Computer programmer
Bob Geldof	Journalist
Debbie Harry	Playboy bunny
Chris Isaak	Tour guide
Mark Knopfler	Journalist
Phil Oakey	Hospital porter
Rod Stewart	Grave digger
Charlie Watts	Graphic artist

— TEN GREAT HIP-HOP 'DISS' RECORDS —

Roxanne Shante – 'Roxanne's Revenge'
A proto-feminist response to UTFO's single about 'Roxanne'
Boogie Down Productions – 'South Bronx'
Answer record to MC Shan's 'The Bridge'. Quarrel over New York's best
hip-hop district ensues
Everlast – 'Whitey's Revenge'
Knocks his fellow white MC Eminem's success
Kool Moe Dee – 'How Ya Like Me Now'
In which he accuses LL Cool J of copying his style...
Luke Campbell (2 Live Crew) – 'Cowards In Compton'
A pop at NWA, it included a video of Dr Dre dressed as a drag queen
Masta Ace – 'So You Wanna Be An MC?'
Clearly aimed at our old friend Puff Daddy
LL Cool J – 'Second Round Knockout'
LL gets his own back on Canibus
2 Pac – 'Hit 'Em Up'
Mr Shakur kindly informs the Notorious BIG that he's
'had' his girlfriend
Ice Cube – 'No Vaseline'
Post-NWA, Ice Cube challenges Eazy-E's sexual orientation
Jay-Z – 'Takeover'
In which he responds to a challenge by Mobb Deep by pointing out one
of the members used to attend ballet lessons

— A BRIEF HISTORY OF DAVID BOWIE—

1947–1966	David Jones (his real name)
1969	Major Tom ('Space Oddity')
1970	Dave in a Dress ('The Man Who Sold The World')
1972	Bowie the Bisexual (1972 *Melody Maker* interview. He later said that he'd lied)
1972–1973	Ziggy Stardust
1974	The Philly Soul Boy (on the *Diamond Dogs* tour)
1976	The Thin White Duke (*Station To Station*) The Man Who Fell To Earth
1980	Major Tom again ('Ashes To Ashes')
1982	Big Suits (The *Serious Moonlight* tour)
1986	The Goblin King (*Labyrinth*)
1989	Tin Machine's lead singer (*Tin Machine*)

— MISSING IN ACTION —

Richie Edwards is perhaps the best-known 'missing in action' rock star. The Manic Street Preacher walked out of the band in February 1995 on the eve of a US tour. His car was found on the banks of the River Severn but despite repeated 'sightings' he has not been found.

Bandleader/ trombonist Glenn Miller's plane disappeared over the English Channel during a flight to Paris for a concert in December 1944. Various conspiracy theories have emerged but the UK Ministry of Defence have agreed that the 'most likely solution' is that his plane was brought down by bombs jettisoned by an RAF plane returning from a mission in Germany.

Original Fleetwood Mac guitarist Jeremy Spencer disappeared in Los Angeles on a US tour in the early '70s, appearing again 5 days later with his head completely shaved. It transpired that he'd joined a religious cult, the Children of God (now known as The Family) which eventually became the title of his 1973 solo album.

Original Pink Floyd member Syd Barrett vanished from public life in the 1970s following a drug-induced breakdown while with the band. His whereabouts are the subject of legend, but he returned to his Cambridge family home, working as a gardener, and although occasionally doorstepped by fans, he hasn't been seen formally in public since.

Joe Strummer disappeared for six weeks in the 1980s. The Clash singer was eventually tracked down in Paris. In his time there he managed to run the Paris marathon without being recognised.

— BEARDS IN ROCK —

ZZ Top
George Michael
Bob Dylan
Liam Gallagher
Bee Gees
Barry White
John Lennon
Jim Morrison
Elvis Costello
Kenny Loggins
Willie Nelson

— SINGLE SALES NEEDED TO REACH NUMBER ONE —

Around a million singles a week have been bought by the British public over the last decade, and traditionally, around 130,000 sales in a week would get you to the top of the charts. 25,000 would see you into the top ten and 6,000 copies shifted would probably be enough to make the top forty. However, in the 21st century, with single sales plummeting wildly, those figures show a major dip.

This trend continues and over 30% less singles were sold in 2003 than in the preceding year. The average weekly sales figure for a number 1 in this year was just 62,000, with around 13,000 sales enough for the top ten and a measly 2,500 copies getting a song into the top forty.

Daniel Bedingfield holds the modern record for the lowest weekly sales of a number 1 record, shifting just 25,000 copies of 'I Gotta Get Through This' and still hitting the top of the charts. 'We're-not-a-boy-band' Busted have the lowest total sales figure for a number 1 – 'Who's David' shifted 71,000 copies during its entire stay in the charts.

— NEWS JOURNALISTS WHO DIG MUSIC —

Krishnan Guru-Murphy (Lloyd Cole)
Tony Wilson (New Order... obviously)
David Frost (Boz Scaggs)
Rageh Omar (Marvin Gaye)
Jeremy Paxman (The Clash)
Jeremy Vine (Elvis Costello)
Katie Derham (prefers classical music)

— PRENTENTIOUS? MOI? —

'When i hurt i hurt from the inside out and constantly run from it throughout the course of its destructive path. the thing i can always expect is the unexpectable. just when a comfort level of confidence comes along is when i could predict the unpredictable is around the corner.' [sic]

Fred Durst. *Source: brainyquote.com, Fred Durst's weblog*

— DANCE GENRES –A BRIEF GUIDE —
PART TWO

House: General term for dance music with a 4/4 beat and solid electronic bassline

Acid House: Variant of house characterised by use of tone generators and filters

Chicago House: Style of house music from Chicago

Deep House: Slow version of house music, often using jazzy samples

Hip House: A mix of hip-hop and house

Techno: Fast (130-140bpm), often atonal music with a 4/4 beat

Detroit Techno: Music in the style of early techno from Detroit

Hardcore Techno: Fast, distorted techno

Trance: A more minimalist, repetitive form of techno. Can be formulaic

Goa Trance: A more underground variation of trance music

Melodic Trance: A less minimalist, more melodic form of trance music

Progressive Trance: A version of trance that seeks to expand the music's boundaries

Psychedelic Trance: a faster (125-150bpm) version of trance

Minimalist Trance: An amalgamation of psychedelic trance and progressive trance

— MUSICIAN'S KIDS (AND WHAT THEY DO) —

Dhani Harrison (George Harrison)	Musician
Enrique Iglesias (Julio Iglesias)	Musician
Julian Lennon (John Lennon)	Musician; restaurant owner
Kelly Osbourne (Ozzy Osbourne)	Musician
Kimberly Stewart (Rod Stewart)	Model
Lisa Marie Presley (Elvis)	Musician
Liv Tyler (Steven Tyler)	Actress
Norah Jones (Ravi Shankar)	Musician
Stella McCartney (Paul McCartney)	Fashion Designer
Ziggy Marley (Bob Marley)	Musician

— COLLABORATIONS FROM BEYOND THE GRAVE —

'A Little Less Conversation'	Elvis Presley and JXL
'All The Way '	Celine Dion and Frank Sinatra
Born Again	Notorious BIG with Eminem, Missy Elliott, Snoop Dogg etc
Chant Down Babylon	Bob Marley with Lauryn Hill, Chuck D, Guru and Aerosmith
'Free As A Bird'	The Beatles
'Have You Ever Been Lonely'	Patsy Cline and Jim Reeves*
Patsy Cline Duets Vol. 1	Patsy Cline with Willie Nelson, Waylon Jennings and Glen Campbell
'Soul Searchin''	Brian Wilson and Carl Wilson
Tupac – Resurrection	Tupac Shakur with Notorious BIG and 50 Cent
'Unbreakable'	Michael Jackson and Notorious BIG
'Unforgettable'	Nat King Cole and Natalie Cole

* *The only collaboration that didn't feature any living performers*

— COMEDIANS IN ROCK —

Harry Enfield – 'Loadsamoney (Doin' Up The House)'
Russ Abbott – 'Atmosphere'
Young Ones with Cliff Richard – 'Livin' Doll'
Mike Reid – 'The Ugly Duckling'
Jasper Carrott – 'Funky Moped'/'Magic Roundabout'
The Goodies – 'The Funky Gibbon'
Benny Hill – 'Ernie (The Fastest Milkman In The West)'
Goons – 'Ying Tang Song'
Monty Python – 'Always Look On The Bright Side Of Life'
Hylda Baker and Arthur Mullard – 'You're The One That I Want'
Billy Connolly – 'D.I.V.O.R.C.E.'
Kenny Everett – 'Snot Rap'

— MUSICAL DISCOVERIES —

Artist	Discovered...
Bessie Smith	Discovered singing in the street by fellow singer Ma Rainey
Frank Sinatra	Discovered by Harry James in 1939 while working as a comedian and MC at an Englewood Cliffs roadhouse
Arthur Conley	Discovered by fellow soul star Otis Redding aged 18
Kriss Kross	Teen hip-hoppers discovered by Jermaine Durpi, himself only 19, when shopping for shoes
Annabelle LuWin (Bow Wow Wow)	Discovered in a laundrette by Malcolm McLaren
Human League	Phil Oakey discovered Suzanne Sulley and Joanne Catherall dancing at a Sheffield disco
Billie	Chris Evans' beau was auditioning as a dancer when she was spotted by a record exec
Jewel	Was playing the coffee houses of Michigan when an Atlantic A&R man spotted her
Altered Images	Clare Grogan was discovered by Bill Forsythe while working as a waitress
The Freshies	Discovered by himself. Chris Sievey's Manchester popsters were dismissed by record companies so often he published a book of rejection slips, and a second book featuring rejections from Virgin Records alone. Eventually scored a hit single when Sievey convinced MCA to give them a chance.

— CLASSIC CHRISTMAS ALBUMS —

Elvis's Christmas Album (recorded in the summer of 1957)
Frank Sinatra: *A Jolly Christmas From Frank Sinatra* (1957)
Nat King Cole: *The Magic Of Christmas* (1960)
Bing Crosby: *I Wish You A Merry Christmas* (1962)
The Beach Boys: *Christmas Album* (1964)
Joan Baez: *Noël* (1966)
Herb Alpert & The Tijuana Brass: *Christmas Album* (1968)
Ella Fitzgerald's Christmas (1968)
Merle Haggard: *Christmas Present* (1973)
Various: *Chistmas Cheers From Motown* (1973)
The Carpenters: *Christmas Portrait* (1978)

— I'M YOUR FAN —

Artist	Inspiration	Fascinating fact
Kurt Cobain	The Raincoats	Kurt was so in love with their album that he came to London to hunt down a vinyl copy and ended up purchasing it from one of the band members
Jaz Coleman	Classical music	Killing Joke's resident shouter now composes classical music
Boy George	Dancehall Reggae	Though he gets fed up with the relentless homophobia, Georgie is a glutton for da riddim riders
John Lydon	Burning Spear	Similarly Mr Rotten himself used to spend most of his punk rock days catching as much of the Jamaican toasters and dub artists as he could
Nick Cave	Johnny Cash	There's little contemporary Mr Cave goes for. He prefers 'storytellers'
Afrika Bambaataa	Gary Numan	Yep, the American hip-hop legend thought Gazza was cool
Charlie Watts	Kenny Clarke	He's really more interested in jazz than brown sugar
Bobby Gillespie	Kylie Minogue	The would-be king of cool latches on to the Antipodean of the delectable derrière.
Marc Bolan	The Damned	The elfin one lurved the new punk music
Jah Wobble	William Blake	London punk geezer sets old Blakey to music

— ROCK 'N' ROLL GIBBERISH —

'Da Doo Ron Ron' – The Crystals
'Ob La Di, Ob La Da' – The Beatles
'Doo Wa Diddy' – Manfred Mann
'De Do Do Do, De Da Da Da' – The Police
'Boom Bang-A-Bang' – Lulu
'Crash! Boom! Bang!' – Roxette
'Rama Lama Ding Dong' – Rocky Sharpe And The Replays
'Da Da Da' – Trio

— ROCKIN' AROUND THE UK —

Number of pages devoted to each county in Pete Frame's *Rockin' Around Britain*, which details the rock 'n' roll landmarks of the UK:

London	47
West Midlands	10
Manchester	9
Surrey	9
Hertfordshire	7
Liverpool	6
Lancashire	5
Buckinghamshire	5
Berkshire	4
Devon	3
Cambridgeshire	3
Cornwall	2
Derbyshire	2
Dorset	2
Cumbria	1
Northumberland	1
Rutland	0
Lincolnshire	0

— TOWARDS AN UNDERSTANDING OF THE MULLET —

The 2003 album *Mullets Rock!* includes tracks by Deep Purple, Alice Cooper, Cheap Trick and The Hollies, thus possibly disproving the maxim, Bad Hair = Bad Music.

On the other hand, a glance down this list of certified mullet-wearers provides ample ammunition:

Billy Rae Cyrus
Kajagoogoo
Michael Bolton
Foreigner
Toto
REO Speedwagon
Wham
Tears For Fears
Spandau Ballet
A Flock Of Seagulls (not strictly a mullet – much, much worse)

— ATTACK OF THE MONDEGREENS —

Probably the most famous of all misheard lyrics (technically known as *mondegreens*) is in Jimi Hendrix's 'Purple Haze'. 'Excuse me while I kiss the sky' does sound suspiciously like 'Excuse me while I kiss this guy'. According to *kissthisguy.com, a website* dedicated to the ancient art of singing incomprehensibly, Hendrix himself was well aware of the confusion and during live performances would wander over to Noel Redding and pretend to kiss him.

Abba wanted their fans to be able to sing along confusion-free, so they enunciated every word terribly clearly – except when it came to 1977's 'Take A Chance On Me', which appeared to feature the following couplets: 'If you change your mind / I'll be upstairs blind / Olly oxen free / Take a chance on me'. Of course, it can be tricky to make out the main vocals over the sound of half the band singing 'Jackie Chan, Jackie Chan, Jackie Chan'.

Some artists, frustrated by the limited opportunities for gibberish offered by their native tongue, switch to something more exotic. John Lennon pioneered this approach in 'Across The Universe', with the line 'Jai guru deva' prompting millions of people to wonder who Jackaroo Dave was. Meanwhile Kula Shaker decided that Sanskrit is the true language of rock'n'roll. A Toronto DJ told the band during an interview that she thought the chorus of 'Tattva' was 'A gingerbread maker made a time bomb.' When, of course, it was really 'Acintya Bheda Bheda Tattva.'

Other memorable mondegreens include:
Ronan Keating, 'Life Is A Rollercoaster':
'Life is a rollercoaster. / I've just got a rabbit'

Robert Palmer, 'Addicted To Love':
'Might as well face it, you're a dickhead in love'

The Beatles, 'I Saw Her Standing There'
'We danced through the night / And we held each other's kite'

The Stone Roses, 'Love Spreads':
'I'm having cheese with a pygmy / She's over there'

Led Zeppelin, 'Whole Lotta Love':
'I'm gonna give you every inch of my gloves'

— TOP TEN SHREDDERS —

The Human League's Martyn Ware once said that they took up keyboards because guitars gave them sore fingers. Pity the Shredders then, guitarists who eschew conventional values of melody and rhythm for speed and dexterity, their music designed only to demonstrate how fast they can get up and down the fretboard.

The top 10 according to *Guitar* magazine:

1. Michael Angelo
2. Chris Impellitteri
3. Yngwie Malmsteen
4. Paul Gilbert (Racer X)
5. Shawn Lane (ex-Black Oak Arkansas)
6. Joe Stump
7. Rusty Cooley
8. Buckethead
9. John Petrucci (Dream Theater)
10. The Great Kat

— NOT TO BE CONFUSED... —

Songs that share titles with other, completely different songs:

Song	Different versions recorded by
'Chocolate'	Kylie Minogue, Snow Patrol
'Come Together'	The Beatles, Primal Scream
'Crazy'	Seal, Aerosmith, Eternal, Patsy Cline, Mud
'Desire'	Talk Talk, U2
'Drive'	REM, The Cars
'High'	The Cure, Feeder, Lighthouse Family
'I'm Free"	Soup Dragons, Roger Daltrey
'Is This Love?'	Alison Moyet, Whitesnake
'Jump'	Van Halen, Pointer Sisters
'Let's Dance'	Five, David Bowie
'One'	U2, Metallica
'The Power Of Love'	Frankie Goes To Hollywood, Jennifer Warnes
'Promises'	Buzzcocks, Take That, Def Leppard
'Time'	Culture Club, Prince
'Without You'	Motley Crue, Nilsson

— I GUESS THAT'S WHY THEY CALL IT THE BOOZE —

Twelve tunes to enjoy a wee drinkie to:

'Cigarettes And Alcohol' – Oasis
'Gin And Juice' – Snoop Doggy Dogg
'Gold Gin' – Kiss
'Lilac Wine' – Jeff Buckley
'Little Old Wine Drinker Me' – Merle Haggard
'Me And My Wine' – Def Leppard
'One Bourbon, One Scotch, One Beer' – George Thorogood
And The Destroyers
'Pass The Courvoisier' – Busta Rhymes
'Streams Of Whiskey' – The Pogues
'Tequila Sunrise' – The Eagles
'Titties 'n' Beer' – Frank Zappa
'Whisky In The Jar' – Thin Lizzy

— MUSIC JOURNALISM —

'Most rock journalism is people who
can't write, interviewing people who
can't talk for people who can't read.'

Frank Zappa

— DEAD RAPPERS —

Big DS (Onyx)	Died of cancer in 2003
Big L	Murdered in 1999
Big Punisher	Died of a heart attack in 2000
Eazy-E (NWA)	Died of AIDS in 1995
Freaky Tah (Lost Boyz)	Murdered in 1999
Jam Master Jay (Run DMC)	Murdered in 2002
Khadafi (Outlawz)	Murdered in 1996
Mista C (RBL Posse)	Killed in a drive-by, 1995
Notorious BIG	Murdered in 1997
Poetic (Gravediggaz)	Died of cancer in 2001
Scott La Rock (KRS-One)	Murdered in 1987
Soulja Slim	Murdered in 2003
Tupac Shakur	Murdered in 1996

— YOU CAN'T SAY THAT ON TV —

The relationship between television and rock has always been a bumpy one: when Elvis first appeared on screen, he was only shown from the waist up to prevent impressionable teenagers from seeing his gyrating hips. But that was nothing compared to the horror of British newspapers when, in 1976, The Sex Pistols appeared on TV with presenter Bill Grundy. Somewhat the worse for wear, guitarist Steve Jones called Grundy a 'dirty f***er' and 'a f***ing rotter'; the following morning, every British newspaper's front page was devoted to the outrage; according to reporters, at least one viewer was so incensed by the Pistols' language that he kicked in his television. The *Daily Mail*'s headline ('The Filth And The Fury') was later used as the title of a Sex Pistols DVD.

Since the Pistols, other TV outrages have seemed rather tame. Channel 4's rock show *The Tube* was cancelled after presenter (and musician) Jools Holland said 'Come on and watch *The Tube*, you groovy f***ers' during a childrens' television advertising break, and its successor *The Word* tried desperately to generate tabloid outrage – although the most outrageous moment on the show was when controversial US rockers L7 appeared and band member Donita Sparks dropped her shorts while on air. Other TV programmes were newsworthy by accident: in 1989, viewers of the sober and serious arts programme *The Late Show* were treated to the sight of The Stone Roses going ballistic and shouting 'amateurs!' at the programme's presenters and technicians after their performance was cut short.

— TEN LEFT-HANDED GUITARISTS —

Albert King
Bob Geldof
David Byrne*
Dick Dale
Jimi Hendrix*
Kurt Cobain
Mark Knopfler*
Paul McCartney
Paul Simon*
Tony Iommi
* *plays a right-handed guitar*

— DOES THE DEVIL HAVE THE BEST TUNES? —

Famously Christian bands and artists:

Creed	Christian nu-metal act, as in 'Oh God, it's Creed'. Denied being a Christian band once successful, and split in 2004.
Delirious?	UK Christian dance/rock band who sell thousands of records with virtually no airplay or mainstream press coverage.
Evanescence	The breakthrough band of 2004 built a strong following in the Christian music scene, but appalled their fans when they reached the mainstream and started displaying some very un-Christian behaviour, such as swearing.
Mortification	The most famous Christian Death Metal band on the planet, probably because nobody can name any other Christian Death Metal bands.
POD	POD is short for 'Payable On Death', as in 'The wages of sin are...'
Stryper	Christian heavy metal band of the mid-'80s, famous for their striped yellow and black spandex. Split in 1991.
U2	Before their second album, U2 nearly split up: they weren't sure whether rock music was an appropriate career for devout Christians.

— ODD VENUES FOR GIGS —

1969: The Beatles, on the roof of Apple Records
1977: Throbbing Gristle's debut gig, the Institute of Contemporary Arts
1990: The Stone Roses, Spike Island
1979: Spandau Ballet, HMS *Belfast*
2004: Paul Weller's tour of 'forests'
2004: Sheryl Crow, on an aeroplane, 35,000ft up
2004: Liberty X, the second Twenty 20 cricket final
2003: Bjork, Coney Island funfair

— BOOKISH BANDS —

Belle and Sebastian	From the French novel of the same name (via its cartoon dramatisation)
Boo Radleys	A character in Harper Lee's *To Kill A Mockingbird*
Depeche Mode	From a French fashion magazine's front cover
Good Charlotte	After the book of the same name
Heaven 17	A band in Anthony Burgess's *A Clockwork Orange*
Joy Division	From *The House Of Dolls*, by Karol Cetinsky
Level 42	From Douglas Adams' *The Hitch-Hiker's Guide To The Galaxy*
Love and Rockets	From the comic book of the same name
Marillion	From Tolkein's *The Silmarillion*
Moloko	The milk bar in *A Clockwork Orange*
Mott The Hoople	From Willard Manus's novel of the same name
Paradise Lost	John Milton's epic poem, *Paradise Lost*
Primal Scream	From Arthur Janov's Primal Scream therapy
Savage Garden	From Anne Rice's *Interview With The Vampire*
Sneaker Pimps	From an article in the Beastie Boys' *Grand Royal* magazine about footwear procurers
Soft Machine	William Burroughs, *The Soft Machine*
Steppenwolf	Herman Hesse, *Steppenwolf*
The Doors	From Aldous Huxley's *The Doors Of Perception*
The Fall	Albert Camus, *The Fall*
The Teardrop Explodes	A line from a *Daredevil* comic
The Velvet Underground	Michael Leigh, *The Velvet Underground*
Uriah Heep	A character in Dickens' *David Copperfield*
Veruca Salt	A character in Roald Dahl's *Charlie And The Chocolate Factory*

— REVIEW OF SPINAL TAP'S *INTRAVENUS DE MILO* —

'This tasteless cover is a good indication of the lack of musical invention within. The musical growth of this band cannot be charted. They are treading water in a sea of retarded sexuality and bad poetry.'

— THE RAINBOW OF ROCK —

Green Day

Yello   **Blue**

Orange Juice   The **Indigo** Girls

Simply **Red**   **Violet** Indiana

— IN BLACK AND WHITE —

Black Rebel Motorcycle Club	Average White Band
Black Sabbath	Whitesnake
Black	White Town
Black Lace	The White Stripes
The Black Crowes	Barry White

— 'A FEW OF MY FAVOURITE THINGS' —

- Raindrops on roses
- Whiskers on kittens
- Bright copper kettles
- Warm woollen mittens
- Brown paper packages tied up with string
- Cream coloured ponies
- Crisp apple strudels
- Doorbells
- Sleigh bells
- Schnitzel with noodles
- Wild geese that fly with the moon on their wings
- Girls in white dresses with blue satin slashes
- Snowflakes that stay on my nose and eyelashes
- Silver white winter that melts into spring

— TEN GREAT INSTRUMENTALS —

'Albatross' – Fleetwood Mac

'Apache' – The Shadows

'Green Onions' – Booker T And The MGs

'Miserlou' – Dick Dale And His Del-Tones

'Oxygene Part IV' – Jean Michel Jarre

'Peter Gunn Theme' – Duane Eddy

'Rumble' – Link Wray

'Song For Guy' – Elton John

'Telstar' – The Tornados

'Wipeout' – The Surfaris

— TEN TERRIBLE RECORDS BY GREAT ARTISTS —

'Wiggle Wiggle', Bob Dylan (*Oh Mercy*)
'Wiggle Wiggle Wiggle like a bowl of soup,' sang the spokesman
for a generation. Oh mercy indeed.

'Miami', U2 (*Pop*)
Pop is arguably U2's biggest mistake, and this mumbling
monstrosity is by far the worst song on it.

'Shiny Happy People', REM (*Out Of Time*)
Thankfully it's been excised from the REM canon (you won't
find it on their recent best-of), because even REM know it's
rubbish.

'Metal Machine Music', Lou Reed (*Metal Machine Music*)
Strangely, an entire album of white noise from rock's Mr Happy
didn't exactly fly off the shelves.

'Batdance', Prince (*Batman*)
The beginning of the end of the purple one's pop career,
'Batdance' was a tune- and idea-free zone.

'Boris The Spider', The Who (*Who's Last*)
Yes, it was the '60s; yes, drugs were probably involved; no,
that's still no excuse.

'Undercover Of The Night', The Rolling Stones (*Undercover*)
The Stones get funky. That's funky in the same way that
geography teachers are funky.

'Black Or White', Michael Jackson (*History*)
'It don't matter if you're black or white' – mmmm...

'Candle In The Wind 97', Elton John (single)
The most nauseating record of all time proves that you can't
underestimate the public's taste: it's the UK's best-selling single
of all time.

'American Life', Madonna (*American Life*)
Madonna raps: 'I drive my Mini Cooper and I'm feeling super
duper.' A nation laughs.

THE ONES THAT GOT AWAY
— MUSICIANS WHO LEFT JUST AS FAME BECKONED —

Andy Couzens	Original singer for The Stone Roses. Left in 1986.
Chad Channing	Nirvana's original drummer; replaced by Dave Grohl just before *Nevermind* took the band into orbit.
Dave Mustaine	The Metallica guitarist left the band after their first album and formed Megadeth, but his band never achieved the same success as his former colleagues.
Henri Padovani	Guitarist for The Police. Left after their first single.
Pete Best	The Beatles ditched their pretty-boy drummer in 1962.
Peter Green	Guitarist Peter Green left Fleetwood Mac in 1970 after announcing that he intended to give all his money away. Bandmate Jeremy Spencer jumped ship the following year.
Steven Duffy	Original singer for Duran Duran. Left in 1979, two years before the band hit the big time.
Syd Barrett	Left Pink Floyd due to drug and/or mental problems. The band recorded *Dark Side Of The Moon* soon afterwards.

— TWENTY ART-ROCKERS —

Blur
Bonzo Dog Doo-Dah Band
The Clash
Chicks On Speed
Franz Ferdinand
Gang Of Four
Ikara Colt
Keith Richards
Pink Floyd
Radiohead
Roxy Music
The Sex Pistols
Stellastarr*
Suede
Talking Heads
The Beatles
The Velvet Underground
The Who
Travis
Wire

— HOW REALITY TV TOOK OVER THE UK CHARTS —

TV talent contests are as old as the hills, but in the early part of the decade a new and much scarier phenomenon developed: reality TV. Bands were no longer formed and discovered, but instead were chosen by the public from a range of wanna-bes and never-gonna-bes. Here are the UK's offerings and details of what happened to each show's winners.

Popstars (2001): The winning wannabes became Hear'Say, a band who quickly discovered the meaning of the phrase 'fickle public'. Derided by the press and abused by strangers in the street, the band broke up in late 2002; singer Mylene Klass is attempting to relaunch herself as a classical musician. The other *Popstars* offshoot, Liberty X, were formed from rejected finalists and have, ironically, had more success than Hear'Say.

Pop Idol (2002): Both Will Young and Gareth Gates captured the nation's hearts, but there could be only one winner – and it was Young, who went on to forge a career as an inoffensive crooner. After a promising start Gates' career headed down the dumper, where – coincidentally – you'll also find the career of fellow finalist and tabloid favourite Darius Danesh.

Fame Academy (2002): The BBC's version of *Pop Idol* introduced the great British public to Scots singer David Sneddon; unfortunately the great British public said 'no thanks' and we haven't heard a peep from him since.

Pop Idol 2 (2003): Series 2's winner was Glaswegian Michelle McManus who, despite constant promotional work on the kiddie-pop circuit, seems destined to be a one hit wonder. A similar fate awaits runners-up Sam and Mark, whose debut single failed to set the world on fire.

Fame Academy Series 2 (2003): The second series of *Fame Academy* was won by Alex Parks, but sadly it seems as if her career will be as spectacular as David Sneddon's: at the time of writing, Parks has had just one minor chart hit.

Popstars: The Rivals (2003): *The Rivals* upped the ante, asking the public to vote on not one, but two brand new bands. The winners – all-girl band Girls Aloud and all-boy band One True Voice – then competed head-to-head for the Christmas number 1, a competition Girls Aloud won with embarrassing ease. The fact that One True Voice were like a less debauched Westlife or Cliff Richard without the raw animal sexuality probably didn't help their chances.

— WHERE THERE'S A HIT, THERE'S A WRIT —

Mike Joyce, drummer with The Smiths, didn't discover until after the band split up that he had only been receiving 10% of the royalties. He sued Morrissey and Johnny Marr, the band's songwriters, and succeeded in winning a more reasonable 25% cut. Delivering his verdict at the High Court, the judge famously described Morrissey as 'devious, truculent and unreliable'.

In their song 'My Book', The Beautiful South borrowed Soul II Soul's famous line 'Back to life, back to reality' – changing the word 'life' to 'bed'. Soul II Soul's songwriter, Jazzy B, sued them and won.

In 1955, Rosa Parks was arrested for refusing to give up her bus seat to a white man, an action that proved instrumental in securing the American civil rights victories of the 1960s. In 1999, she sued Outkast and their record label for releasing a song called 'Rosa Parks', which contained the lyric 'Everybody move to the back of the bus'. She claimed that her name was being exploited and associated with profanity, racism and sexism; she also claimed that the song violated her 'rights of publicity'. On the other side, Outkast claimed the constitutionally guaranteed right to freedom of speech. So far the case has been through four different courts and is still running.

George Michael's record label, Columbia, were taken over by Sony, and things went sour from there. Sony didn't promote George's records the way he wanted them to and a year after the release of *Listen Without Prejudice*, he took Sony to court alleging breach of contract and accusing them of 'professional slavery'. George lost, but later managed to extract himself from his contract. In 2003, he signed a new deal with Sony.

Tony McCarroll, the original drummer with Oasis – who was in the band even before the Gallagher brothers joined – was sacked by Noel in 1995, just as the band were becoming massively successful. Four years later, he sued for unfair dismissal, claiming that he was due a share of any profits resulting from the five-album deal he had signed – even though he only played on one album. He eventually settled out of court for £600,000.

After his solo career took off, Robbie Williams was sued by Take That's manager, Nigel Martin-Smith, who claimed that Robbie had failed to give him six months' notice of his resignation. Robbie claimed that Martin-Smith sacked him, thereby voiding his contract. Robbie lost the case, lost the appeal, and had to pay £90,000 plus a share of his royalties until 2006. His total legal bill was estimated at around £1 million.

— SECRET PSEUDONYMS —

Pseudonym	Better known as...
Bingo Hand Job	REM
Faithless And The Wonderboys	Radiohead
Foregone Conclusion	The Vines
Honking Seals	Pearl Jam
Melvana	Nirvana
The Lemmys	Metallica
The Nobs	Led Zeppelin
The Pump Sounds	The Who
The Seedies	AC/DC
The Spots	The Sex Pistols

— SVENGALIS —

Depending on your point of view svengalis are either pop geniuses, or sinister string-pullers lurking behind the scenes: the hands that rock the cradle or, perhaps, the hands that cradle the rock. No matter what your perspective, though, there's no doubt that the world of music would be a much duller place without the following ten talent spotters:

Svengali	Their charges
Colonel Tom Parker	Elvis
Lou Pearlman	N-Sync, Backstreet Boys
Louis Walsh	Johnny Logan, Boyzone, Girls Aloud
Malcolm McLaren	The Sex Pistols, Bow Wow Wow
Max Martin	Britney Spears, Ace of Base
Simon Cowell	Westlife, The Tweenies, *Pop Idol*
Simon Fuller	Spice Girls, S Club 7, *Pop Idol*
Stock, Aitken And Waterman	Kylie, Jason Donovan, Rick Astley, Sonia
The Matrix	Avril Lavigne
Tom Watkins	East 17, Bros

— THE WIT AND WISDOM OF THE GALLAGHERS — PART FIVE

'I hate the Beach Boys.'
Noel, *Blender* magazine

'If any of them old farts have got a problem with me then leave your zimmer frames at home and I'll hold you up with a good right hook. They're jealous and senile and not getting enough f***ing meat pies.'
Liam on the ex-Beatles, *MTV Europe*

— ROCK STARS AND THEIR PETS —

Star	Species/Breed	Name
Britney Spears	Yorkshire Terrier	*Baby*
Christina Aguilera	Unknown	*Jackson the dog*
Fred Durst	Bulldog	*Bizkit*
Madonna	Chihuahua	*Chiquita*
Ronnie James Dio	Cat	*Jack*
Ryan Peake (Nickelback)	Golden Retriever	*Ben*
Slash	Golden Retriever	*Belle*
Steve Vai	Bees	Names unknown
Will Smith	Rottweilers	*Ludo* and *Zhaki*

Source: VH-1, Lifenetwork.ca

— MOST-PLAYED SONGS ON INTERNATIONAL RADIO —

Over 8 million plays
'You've Lost That Lovin' Feeling' – The Righteous Brothers

Over 7 million plays
'Yesterday' – The Beatles
'Stand By Me' – Ben E King
'(Sittin' On) The Dock Of The Bay' – Otis Redding
'Never My Love' – The Association.

Over 6 million plays
'Mrs Robinson' – Simon And Garfunkel
'Baby I Need Your Loving' – Johnny Rivers
'Georgia On My Mind' – Ray Charles
'Every Breath You Take' – The Police
'Pretty Woman' – Roy Orbison
'Your Song' – Elton John
'Strangers In The Night' – Frank Sinatra
'Breaking Up Is Hard To Do' – Neil Sedaka
'Only You' – The Platters

Over 5 million plays
'Suspicious Minds' – Elvis Presley
'I Will Always Love You' – Dolly Parton
'When A Man Loves A Woman' – Percy Sledge
'Layla' – Derek And The Dominos

— ROCK THE VOTE —

The terminally unfashionable Conservative party have never managed to attract 'hip' artists to their bandwagon – those artists with musical credibility have flocked to movements like Free Nelson Mandela and Rock Against Racism (revitalised in 2004 and supported by new indie stars The Libertines).

Phil Collins famously declared that he would leave the UK if the Labour party got into power. Sadly for all concerned, he didn't keep his promise. Other stars have opted for right-wing ideals. Gary Numan once declared he would vote Tory for the tax breaks, though he has now moved back towards the left and New Labour. Eric Clapton once implored people to vote for Enoch Powell.

Paul Weller eventually got over his union-jack flaunting days in The Jam, when he once advised fans to 'vote Tory', and is now a confirmed socialist and was a major proponent of Red Wedge in the 1980s along with Billy Bragg, The Communards and Madness. Industrial rockers Test Department teamed up with politician Tony Benn to perform the history of the Labour party as a rap at London's *ICA* at a freedom of speech concert which also featured Salman Rushdie reading his *Satanic Verses*.

Meanwhile Simply Red's Mick Hucknall either enhances or diminishes Labour's street cred (depending on your viewpoint) with his backing, while cocktails at Tony Blair's pad as part of the 'Cool Brittania' fad resulted in long-term ridicule.

POP STARS IMMORTALISED IN WAX AT — *MADAME TUSSAUD'S* —

The Spice Girls
Mick Jagger
Sting
Bob Geldof
Michael Jackson
Kylie Minogue
Robbie Williams
Madonna
Britney Spears
Beyoncé

— ROCK STARS' NICKNAMES —

Star	Nickname	Why?
Elvis Presley	*The King*	For services to all the little girls
Keith Moon	*The Loon*	For services to rock 'n' roll mythmaking
John Entwistle	*The Ox*	For his on-stage serenity
Paul Weller	*The Modfather*	For services to the clothes industry
Eric Clapton	*God*	For services to humanity, but more especially blues fans
Paul Hewson	*Bono Vox*	For services to the great tradition of patronising rock stars
James Brown	*Godfather of Soul*	Mrs Brown used to dodge traffic tickets by announcing she had diplomatic immunity due to being married to the Ambassador of Soul. She didn't get off.
Bruce Springsteen	*The Boss*	For services to blue collar rock
Reggie Smalls	*The Notorious BIG* (aka *Biggie*)	For services to takeaway food
Nick Lowe	*Basher*	For 'bashing' them out

— SONGS ABOUT MOVIE STARS —

Kim Carnes – 'Betty Davis Eyes'
Bananarama – 'Robert De Niro's Waiting'
Peter And The Test Tube Babies – 'Elvis Is Dead'
(*'Elvis had a heart attack, because he got too bleedin' fat'*)
Suzanne Vega – 'Marlene On The Wall' (Marlene Dietrich)
MDC – 'John Wayne Was A Nazi'
Elton John – 'Candle In The Wind' (Marilyn Monroe)
Bauhaus – 'Bela Lugosi's Dead'
Prefab Sprout – 'Steve McQueen'
Rufus Wainwright – 'Matinee Idol' (River Phoenix)
Underworld – 'Bruce Lee'
Daniel Bedingfield – 'James Dean (I Wanna Know)'
Daniel Resko – 'Gwyneth Paltrow'

— GUITAR TUNINGS —

The guitar's standard tuning assigns the following notes to the six strings: E A D G B E. It works well most of the time, but most guitarists, sooner or later, experiment with alternate tunings. By retuning certain strings, new chord possibilities and songwriting ideas become available.

Drop D: D A D G B E

Drop D tuning is extremely popular as it makes certain chords much easier but is so similar to standard tuning that it's easy to learn. It was very popular with the grunge bands of the early '90s and was used on Nirvana's 'Heart Shaped Box' and Radiohead's 'Optimistic'.

D Modal: D A D G A D

This tuning works well with Celtic music, but has also been used in rock. Jimmy Page used it on Led Zeppelin's 'Kashmir'.

E Modal: E A D E A E

E modal is used extensively by Martin Carthy.

Open tunings are so called because when the open strings of the guitar are all played together they result in a recognisable chord. They are mainly used by slide guitar players.

Open D: D A D F♯ A D

With open D tuning, strumming the open strings of the guitar gives a D major chord. It was used by The Black Crowes on 'She Talks To Angels'.

Open G: D G D G B D

Open G tunes the guitar to a G major chord. Keith Richards is very fond of open G (though he often removes the bottom string), and used it on 'Honky Tonk Women' and 'Start Me Up'.

Open C: C G C G C E

Tune to a C major chord. Ben Harper used it on 'Breakin' Down'.

Open E Minor: E B E G B E

Open E minor allows the guitarist to switch easily from minor to major chords using just one finger. It was used in early blues playing.

Joni Mitchell claims to have used 51 different guitar tunings during her career.

'PAUL IS DEAD'
— THE BEATLE DEATH CLUES —

On 12 October, 1969, Russell Gibb, a disc jockey for WKNR-FM in Detroit, announced that Paul McCartney was dead. He claimed to have evidence, by which he meant clues sprinkled throughout The Beatles' songs, artwork, and films. The story was picked up by newspapers and TV, and grief swept the US, until it was eventually revealed to be a hoax. Or was it?

To this day, a few fanatics insist that Paul was killed in a car crash in 1966 and that the man known as Paul McCartney is in fact William Campbell, winner of a look-a-like contest that was hushed up.

The clues are, to say the least, exceedingly subtle. Here are just a few of them.

- In 'Yesterday', Paul sings that yesterday came suddenly, that he's no longer the man he used to be, and that there's a shadow hanging over him. And perhaps there is – the shadow of *death*.

- In 'And Your Bird Can Sing', Paul sings 'You can't see me' and 'You can't hear me.' Indeed we can't, because he's *dead*.

- On its front cover, the title of *Rubber Soul* is written in the shape of an upside-down heart. A heart symbolises life. Turn it upside down, and it symbolises *death*.

- In 'Got To Get You Into My Life', Paul sings 'I took a ride, I didn't know what I would find there.' The ride he took was his last one. What he found was *death*.

- On the front cover of *Yesterday And Today*, Paul is sitting inside a trunk. The trunk can only symbolise one thing: a *coffin*.

- Another obvious coffin symbol is the Yellow Submarine. It is in a sea of green, meaning it is underneath the grass, buried. The land of submarines is, therefore, a *cemetery*.

- The title of 'Tomorrow Never Knows' is taken from the *Tibetan Book Of The Dead*. One of the lyrics of the song is 'Play the game of existence to the end.' This can mean only one thing.

- On the famous front cover of *Sergeant Pepper's Lonely Hearts Club Band*, is a small statue of the Hindu god Shiva the Destroyer. His hand points directly at Paul, who is the only member of the band holding a black instrument. Black is the colour of *death*.

- On the back cover of *Sergeant Pepper*, there is a photo of the band. John, George and Ringo are facing the camera, but all we see of Paul is the back of his head. This signifies that the man in the photo is an *imposter*.

- In 'A Day In The Life', John sings 'He blew his mind out in a car. He didn't notice that the lights had changed.' He is describing the death of his friend and colleague.

- Right at the end of 'All You Need Is Love', John sings a phrase that sounds a bit like 'Yes, he's dead.'

- On the front cover of *Abbey Road* and in the booklet that came with the original *Magical Mystery Tour* LP, Paul is barefoot. In Europe, the dead are traditionally buried without shoes.

- At the very end of 'I'm So Tired', there is some mumbling from John. Played backwards, it sounds like 'Paul is dead, man. Miss him, miss him, miss him.'

— TEN ALBUMS PRODUCED BY BRIAN ENO—

Devo – *Q: Are We Not Men? A: We Are Devo!*

Brian Eno – *Here Come The Warm Jets*

Brian Eno – *Ambient 1: Music For Airports*

Robert Fripp And Brian Eno – *No Pussyfooting*

James – *Laid*

Sinéad O'Connor – *Faith And Courage*

Passengers – *Passengers: Original Soundtracks 1*

Talking Heads – *Fear Of Music*

U2 – *The Joshua Tree*

Ultravox – *Ultravox*

— ROCKUMENTARIES —

Title	Subject
A Hard Day's Night	The Beatles*
Biggie & Tupac	Biggie Smalls and Tupac Shakur
Catch A Fire	Bob Marley And The Wailers
Don't Look Back	Bob Dylan
Gimme Shelter	The Rolling Stones
I Am Trying To Break Your Heart	Wilco
If I Should Fall From Grace	Shane McGowan
Kurt & Courtney	Kurt Cobain
Let It Be	The Beatles
Live Forever	Oasis, Blur, Pulp
Madonna: Truth Or Dare	Madonna
Meeting People Is Easy	Radiohead
Nobody Someday	Robbie Williams
Rattle & Hum	U2
Teenage Kicks	The Undertones
The Decline Of Western Civilisation Part I and II	Various punk and metal bands
The Filth And The Fury	The Sex Pistols
The Kids Are Alright	The Who
The Last Waltz	The Band

* combines real and fake documentary footage

— TAT'S ENTERTAINMENT: TATTOOS OF THE STARS — PART THREE

Richie Sambora (Bon Jovi)
Guitar with wings on right arm, cross and roses with GOD above and FAITH below on left upper arm, small star on right hand

Britney Spears
Fairy tattoo on lower back, small daisy circling second toe on right foot, butterfly leaving a vine on left foot, flower with Chinese symbol for mystery in middle on lower stomach. Three Hebrew characters on back of neck, pair of pink dice inside left wrist

Michael Stipe (REM)
1920s cartoon characters Ignatz Mouse and Krazy Kat on underside of right upper arm, small flower design on right hand below thumb

— DON'T GIVE UP THE DAY JOB —
Eight musicians with less than stellar acting careers:

Bono: Not content with a co-writing credit for *The Million Dollar Hotel*, Bono also played the pivotal part of Man In Hotel Lobby. What do you mean, you don't remember it?

Madonna: Madonna has starred in a number of films, and she was rotten in all of them: *Swept Away*, *Body Of Evidence*, *A League Of Their Own*, *Evita*, *Who's That Girl*...

Phil Collins: Determined to prove that he could be annoying on screen as well as on stage, Collins took the lead role in so-so comedy *Buster*.

Elvis: Perhaps it was drugs, or perhaps it was the malign influence of manager Tom Parker. Either way, Elvis performed in some 31 movies, few of which were any good.

Mick Jagger: Old fish-lips has made the odd good film – *Performance* and, er, that's about it – but he's also been utterly wooden in such masterpieces as sci-fi disaster *Freejack* and period piece *Ned Kelly*.

David Bowie: The only memorable thing about Bowie's role as The Goblin King in forgettable fantasy farrago *Labyrinth* was his frightwig, which may have been borrowed from Tina Turner.

Sting: To be fair, Sting has played some impressive roles; then again, he also starred in the confused sci-fi romp *Dune*, in which he donned giant blue pants.

Joe Strummer: The Clash may well have been the finest rock band of all time, but frontman Joe Strummer was a really, really bad actor. Check out *Straight To Hell* if you don't believe us.

MEMBERS OF NEWPORT RAP COLLECTIVE
— *GOLDIE LOOKIN CHAIN* —

Two Hats • Adam Hussein • Mike Balls • Mr Love Eggs
• Mystikal • Billy Webb • Xain • Maggot

— SUPERGROUPS —

Asia	Steve Howe (Yes), Geoff Downes (Buggles), Carl Palmer (ELP), John Wetton (UK)
Audioslave	Chris Cornell (Soundgarden) and Rage Against The Machine
Blind Faith	Eric Clapton, Ginger Baker, Stevie Winwood, Rick Grech (Family)
Cream	Eric Clapton, Jack Bruce and Ginger Baker
Crosby, Stills, Nash and Young	David Crosby (The Byrds), Steven Stills (Buffalo Springfield), Graham Nash (The Hollies) and Neil Young
Derek And The Dominos	Eric Clapton, Duane Allman
Electronic	Bernard Sumner (New Order), Johnny Marr (The Smiths), Neil Tennent (Pet Shop Boys)
Neurotic Outsiders	Steve Jones (The Sex Pistols), Matt Sorum and Duff McKagan (Guns 'N' Roses), John Taylor (Duran Duran)
Notting Hillbillies	Mark Knopfler, Steve Phillips, Brendan Croker, Ed Bicknell, Guy Fletcher, Paul Franklin and Marcus Cliff
Ringo Starr & His All-Starr Band	Ringo Starr, Gary Brooker (Procol Harum), Jack Bruce, Simon Kirke (Free/Bad Company), Todd Rundgren
The Faces	Rod Stewart, Ron Wood, Ronnie Lane, Kenny Jones, Ian McLaglan
The Highwaymen	Willie Nelson, Johnny Cash, Kris Kristofferson and Waylon Jennings
The Jeff Beck Group	Jeff Beck, Rod Stewart, Ron Wood, Mick Waller and Nicky Hopkins
The Power Station	Robert Palmer, John and Andy Taylor (Duran Duran), Tony Thompson (Chic)
Travelling Wilburys	Bob Dylan, Jeff Lynne, Tom Petty, Roy Orbison and George Harrison
Velvet Revolver	Scott Weiland (Stone Temple Pilots), Slash, Duff McKagan and Matt Sorum (Guns 'N' Roses) and Dave Kushner (Wasted Youth)

— EAT TO THE BEAT —

Restaurants and their famous proprietors:

Oko, Glasgow	Jim Kerr, Simple Minds (sold his stake in 2004)
Clarence Hotel, Dublin	Bono and The Edge
Chi, Hollywood	Justin Timberlake (co-owner)
La Boca del Conga Room	Jennifer Lopez (co-owner)
Madre's, Pasadena	Jennifer Lopez
Mountblue, Boston	Steven Tyler & Joe Perry
Century, London	Robbie Williams (co-owner)
Justin's, New York	P Diddy
Man Ray, Paris	Mick Hucknall (co-owner)
Harrington Club, Kensington	Ronnie Wood
The Grit, Athens, Georgia	Michael Stipe
Kaffeebarinn, Reykjavik	Damon Albarn

— SPORTING CONNECTIONS —

Band	Track	Theme tune to:
Fleetwood Mac	'The Chain'	BBC Grand Prix coverage
U2	'Beautiful Day'	ITV's *The Premiership*
Blur	'Song 2'	Ice hockey
Chumbawamba	'Tubthumping'	American football
Booker T And The MGs	'Soul Limbo'	BBC cricket
Lou Bega	'Mambo No. 5'	Channel 4 cricket
Doug Wood Band	'Drag Racer'	BBC snooker
Lightning Seeds	'Life Of Riley'	BBC *Match Of The Day*

— NUMBER OF NUMBER ONE SINGLES PER YEAR —

1960: 17
1970: 14
1980: 24
1990: 18
2000: 42

— ELVIS'S TOP FIVE SINGLES —

Track	Year	Chart peak
'Heartbreak Hotel'	1956	2
'Hound Dog'	1956	2
'All Shook Up'	1957	1
'Teddy Bear'	1957	3
'Party'	1957	2
'Jailhouse Rock'	1958	1
'Don't'	1958	2
'Wear My Ring Around Your Neck'	1958	3
'Hard Hearted Woman'	1958	2
'King Creole'	1958	2
'One Night'	1959	1
'A Fool Such As I'	1959	1
'A Big Hunk O' Love'	1959	4
'Stuck On You'	1960	3
'The Girl Of My Best Friend'	1960	2
'It's Now Or Never'	1960	1
'Are You Lonesome Tonight?'	1961	1
'Wooden Heart'	1961	1
'Surrender'	1961	1
'(Marie's The Name) His Latest Flame'	1961	1
'Can't Help Falling In Love'	1962	1
'Good Luck Charm'	1962	1
'She's Not You'	1962	1
'Return To Sender'	1962	1
'(You're The) Devil In Disguise'	1962	1
'Crying In The Chapel'	1965	1
'In The Ghetto'	1969	2
'Suspicious Minds'	1969	2
'The Wonder Of You'	1970	1
'My Boy'	1974	5
'Way Down'	1977	1
'It's Only Love' / 'Beyond The Reef'	1980	3
'A Little Less Conversation'*	2002	1
'Rubberneckin''**	2003	5
'That's All Right'	2004	3

*(remixed by JXL)
**(remixed by Paul Oakenfold)

— THE BRITS —

Since their inception in 1996 The Brits have honoured the good and the not-so-good of UK music. Winners and losers have included:

WINNERS

Travis	*Best Group* in 2000 and 2002, with Coldplay taking the same award in 2001 and 2003.
Oasis	First winners of *Best British Group*.
Robbie Williams	Three-time winner of *Best UK Male* (1999, 2001 and 2002).
Dido	The most successful female artist with a total of six awards including a brace of *Best Female Solo Artist* gongs.

LOSERS

Craig David	Nominated in six categories in 2001 and failed to win any
Gorillaz	Had the same fate befall them the following year.

— BIGGEST SELLING SOUNDTRACKS OF ALL TIME —

1	*The Bodyguard* (1992)	16 times Platinum
2	*Saturday Night Fever* (1977)	15 times Platinum
3	*Purple Rain* (1984)	13 times Platinum
4	*Forrest Gump* (1994)	12 times Platinum
5	*Dirty Dancing* (1987)	11 times Platinum
=	*Titanic* (1997)	11 times Platinum
6	*The Lion King* (1994)	10 times Platinum
7	*Top Gun* (1986)	9 times Platinum
8	*Grease* (1978)	8 times Platinum
=	*Footloose* (1984)	8 times Platinum
9	*Waiting To Exhale* (1997)	7 times Platinum

— A BIZARRE GARDENING ACCIDENT —

In August 1992 Toto drummer Jeff Porcaro spent an afternoon spraying his garden with chemical poison. Shortly before dinner he was taken ill and later died in hospital. An autopsy also revealed traces of cocaine in his system.

— MUST-HAVE ROCK BIOGRAPHIES —

The Dirt
Motley Crue's account of their debauched career is a
sobering – but very funny – look at what happens
when very stupid men make an awful lot of money.
Possibly the funniest music book ever written.

Last Train From Memphis / Careless Love
Peter Guralnick's epic studies of Elvis Presley are the
definitive biographies of The King, avoiding scurrilous
scandal-mongering without glossing over Elvis's many
faults.

Revolution In The Head
The late Ian MacDonald's exhaustive look at the
Beatles is the definitive rock biography, a truly awe-
inspiring collection of Beatles insider information.

Our Band Could Be Your Life
Michael Azzerad's look at the US underground scene
is a fascinating examination of the US hardcore punk
scene, featuring artists such as Black Flag, Husker Du
and Fugazi.

Hammer Of The Gods
Stephen Davis's account of life on the road with Led
Zeppelin is hugely controversial – it's alleged that
Davis either exaggerates or makes things up
completely – but it's compelling, debauched stuff
nonetheless.

This Is Pop
Ed Jones is a British musician who never quite made it,
and his account of the travails of a mid-level musician
are funny and sad in equal measure. The book's hard
to find but it's well worth tracking down.

REM: Fiction, An Alternative Biography
David Buckley's definitive account of REM's history is
fascinating for fans and non-fans alike.

Head-On/Repossessed
Everyone's favourite rock nutter Julian Cope spills the beans on life before the Teardrop Explodes and the difficulties of being Britain's best loved druid.

Everything (A Book About Manic Street Preachers)
Former *Melody Maker* writer Simon Price's love for the Manics is obvious, and his account of the band's history is often harrowing – especially in the sections about missing guitarist Richey Edwards.

The Mansion On The Hill
Fred Goodman captures the moment when music began to turn into the billion-dollar industry it is today, focusing on artists such as Bob Dylan, Neil Young, Bruce Springsteen and record mogul David Geffen.

— GAMEKEEPER TURNED POACHER —

Musicians that have ended up playing records on the radio:

Marc Reilly	Actually, any life would be easier than sharing a stage with Mark E Smith in The Fall
Jimmy Young	Went from torturing us with his singing to sucking up to Margaret Thatcher
Tom Robinson	Moving from being 'Glad To Be Gay' to a father was an easy step compared to taking up a Radio 6 job
Bruce Dickinson	The Iron Maiden singer, champion fencer and author adds another string to his bow
Manda Rin	Ex-bis (the first unsigned band to appear on *Top Of The Pops*), Amanda MacKinnon changed her name and her job
Brinsley Ford	The ex-Aswad man was already a TV star on *Double Deckers*
Lauren Laverne	The ex-Kenickie songstress now holds down the drivetime slot on London's indie station XFM

— TEN FUNERAL CLASSICS —

1.	'My Heart Will Go On'	Celine Dion
2.	'Candle In The Wind'	Elton John
3.	'The Wind Beneath My Wings'	Bette Midler
4.	'Search For The Hero'	M-People
5.	'My Way'	Frank Sinatra
6.	'You'll Never Walk Alone'	Rogers & Hammerstein
7.	'Please Release Me'	Engelbert Humperdinck
8.	'Memory'	Elaine Page
9.	'Strangers In The Night'	Frank Sinatra
10.	'Bright Eyes'	Art Garfunkel

Source: Co-operative Funeral Society

— MUSICAL FAMILIES —

The Jacksons
The Bee Gees (Gibb family)
The Corrs
The Nolan Sisters
The Partridge Family
The Everly Brothers
The Osmonds
Five Star (Steadman family)
Hanson
The Carpenters
Bros (Matt and Luke Goss)

— PRETENTIOUS? MOI? —
PART THREE

'U2 is an original species... there are colours and feelings and emotional terrain that we occupy that is ours and ours alone.'
Bono

'I'm an ocean, because I'm really deep. If you search deep enough you can find rare exotic treasures.'
Christina Aquilera

'I feel safe in white because deep down inside, I'm an angel.'
P Diddy

— APPLE VS APPLE —

In 1968, The Beatles founded their own record company, Apple Corps, to release their records and handle all their business affairs. To this day, Apple control the rights to all The Beatles' recordings. In 1977, Apple Computers was founded. Three years later, George Harrison saw an advert for Apple Computers in a magazine, and battle commenced. Apple Computers and Apple Corps have now been fighting over their trademarks for a staggering 24 years – and they still haven't finished.

It all started out quite agreeably. In 1981, after a long negotiation, the two firms agreed that Apple Corps would use the name Apple in the entertainment industry and Apple Computer would use it in the computer industry. At the time, no-one had any idea that the two industries would converge. However, by 1987, Apple's computers had sound capabilities, so the firm sought to negotiate a new agreement. They failed.

Despite this, Apple Computer started to equip their machines with MIDI, the universal language for electronic musical instruments. In 1989, Apple Corps asked them to withdraw the MIDI-equipped machines. They refused, and their lawyers spent the next two years in London's High Court, plus ten days in the Court of Appeal and one day in Brussels. In 1991, the two sides reached an agreement. The details were never disclosed, but analysts believe that Apple Computer paid Apple Corps about $30 million and, crucially, the new agreement, just like the old one, stated that Apple Computer had to keep their brand name out of the record industry.

All was well until 2003, when Apple launched the iTunes music store, effectively turning themselves into a record company, and ran an advertising campaign using the brand name *AppleMusic*. On 25 February 2004, the two firms went back to court in London, and the case is expected to drag on for years. According to Fox News, a spokesman for Apple Corps said, 'It's OK with us if they want to go this route. It's just more money for us.'

— CHEAPSKATES —

When Decca famously turned down The Beatles, it was in favour of Brian Poole And The Tremeloes who were selected because of their superior performance at an audition (The Beatles had partied until 4:30 am that morning), and because The Tremeloes lived just a mile away and would cost the company less in travel expenses.

— BLACK MUSIC FOR WHITE PEOPLE —

Since the 1930s, black American musicians had been playing the blues, but when Chuck Berry sped up the classic 12-bar and starting singing about his main loves – girls and cars – a new phenomenon was born. This music started to appeal to a wider audience but while Berry, Little Richard and Fats Domino were inventing rock 'n' roll, the industry was lining up a conveyor belt of white singers to take it to the heart of Middle America. So who were the Eminems of their day?

Bill Haley
Originally a B-side, 'Rock Around The Clock' by Bill Haley And His Comets featured in the 1955 film *Blackboard Jungle* and became an overnight sensation. The film and the song switched Middle America on to a new sound and could be said to be the birth of rock 'n' roll as a global phenomenon.

Jerry Lee Lewis
Raised in an extremely religious family, Jerry grew up listening to blues, country and gospel. After being expelled from bible school for 'boogying up' the hymns, he started to combine the music he loved into his own distinctive style, based on raw energy. Breakthrough hit 'Whole Lot Of Shakin' Goin' On' hit number 1 in the pop, country and blues charts.

Pat Boone
Boone, along with the likes of Paul Anka and Bobby Darin, presented a 'cleaned-up' form of rock 'n' roll that rejected some of its more risqué elements and had more in common with the crooning balladeers of the '40s. Boone would often release sanitised cover versions of songs by the likes of Little Richard, and although not held in high esteem by teenagers, he was more popular with parents.

Elvis Presley
There's not much to say about the man known simply as 'The King' that hasn't been said before. Singing raunchy rock 'n' roll songs with a curl of the lip and a wiggle of the hips that had parents outraged, Elvis hit the charts in 1956 with 'Heartbreak Hotel' and the legend was born.

Buddy Holly
Holly's popularity rivalled Elvis in the 1950s before his tragic death in a plane crash in 1959 at the age of just 22. Among the first rock artists to be heavily involved in all aspects of his music including writing and production, hits like 'Peggy Sue' and 'That'll Be The Day' offered a new slant on rock 'n' roll.

— SHOT AND SURVIVED —

50 Cent	Shot nine times in 2000
Ace Frehley (Kiss)	Accidentally shot himself with an Uzi, 1998
Bob Marley	Unsuccessful assassination attempt, 1976
Bushwick Bill	Had an eye shot out by his girlfriend, 1991
Dusty Hill (ZZ Top)	Accidentally shot himself in the stomach, 1984
Ol' Dirty Bastard (Wu Tang Clan)	Shot by burglars, 1998
Ray Davies (The Kinks)	Shot in the leg while chasing a mugger, 2004
Scarface (Geto Boys)	Shot by a policeman, 1993
Tim Westwood (Radio 1)	Shot by bikers in London, 1999
Tupac Shakur*	Shot in a robbery, 1994*

* *Tupac was shot again in a drive-by two years later. This time he didn't survive.*

— P.S. I LOVE YOU —

Song	Artist	About
'American Pie'	Don McLean	Buddy Holly
'How Do You Sleep?'	John Lennon	Paul McCartney
'Jean Genie'	David Bowie	Iggy Pop
'Killing Me Softly'	Roberta Flack	Don McLean
'Layla'	Eric Clapton	George Harrison's wife, Patti
'Nightshift'	The Commodores	Marvin Gaye, Jackie Wilson
'Shine On You Crazy Diamond'	Pink Floyd	Syd Barrett
'Stuck In A Moment You Can't Get Out Of'	U2	Michael Hutchence
'The Whole Of The Moon'	The Waterboys	Prince
'You're So Vain'	Carly Simon	Warren Beatty*

* *allegedly – Simon's keeping schtum*

THE MOST RIDICULOUS STAGE PROPS
— OF ALL TIME—

Cannons
A key component of any AC/DC show

Eddie
Iron Maiden's giant – and let's face it, not very scary –
on-stage monster

German cars
U2's 1992 *Zoo TV* tour featured suspended Trabant
cars, which had been converted into spotlights

Giant inflatable penis
The Beastie Boys' fourth, ahem, member in early tours

Giant inflatable pig
Originally featured on the cover of Pink Floyd's
Animals, and then used at gigs

Giant inflatable women
The Rolling Stones' prop for live renditions of 'Honky
Tonk Women'

Giant Lemon
U2 got trapped in their giant lemon during the *Popmart*
tour, 1997

Live Cattle
ZZ Top once toured with an entire menagerie on stage

Rotating Drum Kit
Not the brightest idea, as Motley Crue drummer Tommy
Lee discovered when he fell out of his upside-down kit

World War 2 Bomber
Touring their *Bomber* album, Motorhead's lighting rig
was a mock-up of a Lancaster bomber. According to
rock legend, when the band played in Dresden singer
Lemmy told the crowd: 'Good evening, Dresden. I bet
you haven't seen one of these for a while.'

— BANDS FROM ONE TO 10,000 —

A1
One Dove
U2
2Unlimited
The 3 Degrees
The 4 Of Us
5 Star
5ive
The Dave Clark Five
The Jackson Five
Maroon 5
The MC5
S Club 7
10CC
East 17
UB40
Level 42
JJ72
Haircut 100
Blink 182
The 411
911
1927
Bran Van 3000
10000 Maniacs

— BEFORE THEY WERE FAMOUS... —

Rat Scabies and Captain Sensible (The Damned): Toilet cleaners in Croydon
Dave Vanian (The Damned): Gravedigger
Billy Bragg: Squaddie
Mick Jagger: Porter at a mental hospital
Feargal Sharkey (The Undertones): TV repairman
Martin Newell (The Cleaners From Venus): Landscape gardener
Elvis Costello: Computer programmer
Madonna: Used to work at Dunkin' Donuts in Times Square
Peter Gabriel: Made hats
Henry Rollins: Sold ice cream
Jet Black (The Stranglers): Sold ice cream

— MUSICAL SPORTS FANS —

Ed from Radiohead	The only 'sporty' one in everyone's favourite Oxford miserabilists supports the 'dark side'. That's Manchester United to me and you
Badly Drawn Boy	Had trials for Manchester United
Skids	Both Richard Jobson and Stuart Adamson were fans of Dunfermline Athletic FC and they regularly play 'Into The Valley' at home games
Hugh Cornwell (Stranglers)	Once organised a rock bands versus journalists cricket match
Gil Scott Heron	His father played for Celtic
Des O'Connor	Was on Northampton Town's books
Sean Paul	Represented Jamaica at water polo
Sammy Hagar	His father was boxer Bobby Burns
Julio Iglesias	Before a car accident, stood between the sticks for Real Madrid
MC Hammer	Was named during a stint as ball boy for the Oakland Athletics
Bob Willis	Adopted middle name 'Dylan' in tribute to his hero

ACTORS FROM *NEIGHBOURS* WHO HAVE — GONE ON TO HAVE POP CAREERS —

Kylie Minogue
Jason Donovan
Craig McLachlan
Stefan Dennis
Natalie Imbruglia
Holly Valance
Delta Goodrem

— MIND CONTROL —

The Shamen claimed that they incorporated special brainwave patterns into their electronic music programming to put listeners into a joyful, hypnotic, Shamen-loving trance. Considering how many people hate their music, this may be a lie.

— *TOP OF THE POPS* THEME TUNES —

Top Of The Pops is a British institution, as important as the Queen, fish and chips, *Coronation Street* and Elton John to British culture. The various theme tunes and the title sequences that went with them have always been talking points. Who could forget the psychedelic dancing girls of the early '70s, or the records that looked as if they were going to fly straight out of the screen?

The original *TOTP* theme tune was 'Percussion Piece' by John Stewart and Harry Rabonowitz, replaced in 1972 by Led Zeppelin's 'Whole Lotta Love'. It wasn't until 1981 that the titles had a revamp, with 'Yellow Pearl' by Thin Lizzy's Phil Lynott replacing the Zep, accompanied by the classic 'flying records' title sequence. It was all change again in 1986 when *TOTP* recruited 'N-n-n-n-nineteen' composer Paul Hardcastle to write a theme that would be up to speed with the new electronic sounds of the '80s. The result was the hard-hitting electro-pop gem 'The Wizard,' a good match for the neon armageddon of a title sequence that accompanied it.

This lasted until 1991, when it too was replaced, this time by 'Now Get Out Of That' by Tony Gibber. Erasure's Vince Clarke tried his hand, and his 'Red Hot Pop' remained the theme tune for three years, from 1995 to 1998, before the post-modern geniuses at the BBC brought back 'Whole Lotta Love', remixed by Bad Man Bad. This rather frightening version took the hard rock classic off in a new psychotic lounge direction and is still the theme tune for *TOTP*'s sister show *Top Of The Pops 2*, though a remix of Gibber's 'Now Get Out Of That' returned to the main show in its latest revamp in 2003.

— RECORDS BANNED DURING THE GULF WAR —

Abba – 'Waterloo'
Bangles – 'Walk Like An Egyptian'
The Beatles – 'Back In The USSR'
Phil Collins – 'In The Air Tonight'
Cutting Crew – 'I Just Died In Your Arms Tonight'
Duran Duran – 'A View To A Kill'
Eddie Grant – 'Living On The Frontline'
Elton John – 'Saturday Night's Alright For Fighting'
Donny Osmond – 'Soldier Of Love'
Bruce Springsteen – 'I'm On Fire'
Status Quo – 'In The Army Now'
10CC – 'Rubber Bullets'

— WHAT DO YOU MEAN, THE GIG'S CANCELLED? —

1977: Several dates on The Sex Pistols' *Anarchy In The UK* tour were pulled due to complaints from local councillors.

1998: The Rolling Stones pulled a whole UK tour because they were worried about paying tax.

1999: Morrissey cancelled a show in Dresden when he realised it was due to take place in a converted slaughterhouse.

1999: Marilyn Manson's show at Red Rocks was pulled by local officials after the Columbine massacre.

2002: Oasis had to pull out of Indianapolis gigs after Noel Gallagher and two other band members were injured in a car crash.

2003: Van Morrison pulled out of a gig at the Royal Crown Hotel in Wiltshire and was promptly sued for £500,000 by the landlord for injury to his reputation.

2004: Beenie Man's gigs in the UK were pulled after Peter Tatchell and others accused him of homophobia.

— ROCK'S TOP TEN PREACHERS —

Al Green
Little Richard
Sinead O'Connor
The Singing Nun
Reverend Run (of Run DMC)
Bishop Jeff Banks
Reverend Julius Cheeks
Reverend James Cleveland
'Saint' Cliff Richard
The Osmonds
(they now run a Christian-themed family theatre in Missouri)

— THE COMEBACK KIDS —

Artist	Split up in	Comebacks
The Who	1978	Have been going intermittently ever since
Madness	1986	Reformed for Madstock in 1992
Black Sabbath	1979	Continuied after Ozzy left with Ronnie James Dio, before Oz came back on board for *Live Aid*, although he didn't rejoin properly until 1997
The Sex Pistols	1978	Reformed in 1996, for the money
The Foundations	1970	Reformed a year later and have toured ever since
Dead Kennedys	1986	Reformed without Jello Biafra in 21st century to everyone's disappointment, not least Biafra's
Culture Club	1986	Reunion attempt four years later failed in 1990, began working together again in 1997

— SONGS ABOUT PROSTITUTION —

'Bad Girls'	Donna Summer
'Candy's Room'	Bruce Springsteen
'Charlotte The Harlot'	Iron Maiden
'Honky Tonk Women'	The Rolling Stones
'House Of The Rising Sun'	The Animals
'Lady Marmalade'	Labelle
'Maggie Mae'	The Beatles
'Maggie M'Gill'	The Doors
'Mama'	Genesis
'Private Dancer'	Tina Turner
'Roxanne'	The Police
'Ruby Don't Take Your Love To Town'	Kenny Rogers
'St Teresa'	Joan Osborne

— GIGS FROM HELL —

When you consider the things that can go wrong at concerts – a volatile mix of hundreds or thousands of people, alcohol and drugs, pyrotechnics. and idiots – it's not a surprise that things occasionally go wrong. But while the majority of shows go without a hitch, some concerts were truly disastrous.

The most famous rock disaster was Altamont in 1969, where 18-year-old Meredith Hunter died during a Rolling Stones performance. The security – Hell's Angels – beat Hunter to death, and three other people also died at the concert. Altamont is now seen as the day when peace and love turned much, much nastier.

Some disasters inspired music: an early '70s show at the Montreux Casino by Frank Zappa And The Mothers Of Invention was cut short when a fan fired a flare gun at the ceiling, and the venue burned to the ground. The fire inspired heavy rockers Deep Purple, who wrote 'Smoke On The Water' about it.

Sadly not all shows are so inspiring: the 1999 Woodstock festival was marred by violence including arson, riots and rapes, while the following year nine fans were crushed to death when the crowd pushed forward during a Pearl Jam performance at Denmark's Roskilde festival. Then in 2003, 97 people died in a US nightclub during a performance by rock band Great White. Like many such tragedies, it was utterly preventable: the band's pyrotechnics ignited the venue, turning the club into an inferno in a matter of seconds.

— THE WIT AND WISDOM OF THE GALLAGHERS — PART SIX

'He's just an old git.'
Noel on David Bowie, source unknown

'What a bunch of miserable, moaning f***ers.'
Oasis on Starsailor, *NME*

'Just because you sell a lot of records it doesn't mean you're any good. Just look at Phil Collins.'
Liam, Patrick Kielty's *Almost Live* show

'They don't do anything. Make a record, you lazy bastards!'
Liam on the Rolling Stones, *NME*

— DANCE GENRES – A BRIEF GUIDE —
PART THREE

Electronica: Generic term for all kinds of electronic music, particularly abstract/experimental

Big Beat: Breakbeat rhythms and unusual samples, popularised by The Chemical Brothers and Fatboy Slim

Hardcore: Very fast dance music, usually computer-generated, with speeds up to 300bpm

Gabba: Loud and aggressive counterpoint to happy hardcore

Happy Hardcore: Very fast techno with speeded up vocals

Hi-NRG: An evolution of disco, with faster rhythms and a strong cheese factor

Garage: More soulful, gospel-tinged form of house

Speed Garage: UK garage variant featuring half-tempo basslines

UK Garage: Another name for speed garage, named after the Paradise Garage club

Industrial: Aggressive mix of rock and techno

Rave: A derivative of Acid House that accompanied 1990s 'raves'

Electroclash: 1990s update of electropop

Electropop: 1980s pop music characterised by a cold, robotic sound

Synthpunk: Late '70s punk played using synthesisers instead of guitars

Intelligent Dance Music: Experimental dance music. Usually impossible to dance to.

— TEN ADULTERER'S ANTHEMS —

'The Dark End Of The Street'	James Carr
'Norwegian Wood'	The Beatles
'So Hard'	Pet Shop Boys
'Always The Last To Know'	Del Amitri
'Into Temptation'	Crowded House
'I Heard It Through The Grapevine'	Marvin Gaye
'Careless Whisper'	George Michael
'Cry Me A River'	Justin Timberlake
'It Wasn't Me'	Shaggy
'Cheating On You'	Franz Ferdinand

— DRUGS —

Song	Artist	About
'Eight Miles High'	The Byrds	Amphetamines
'Scooby Snacks'	Fun Loving Criminals	Barbiturates
'Cocaine'	Eric Clapton	Cocaine
'Street Lobotomy'	Body Count	Crack
'Dr Feelgood'	Motley Crue	Drug dealers
'Dr Robert'	The Beatles	Drug dealers
'Ebeneezer Goode'	The Shamen	Ecstasy
'Sorted for E's and Whizz'	Pulp	Ecstasy, Amphetamines
'Cold Turkey'	John Lennon	Heroin
'Don't Bring Harry'	The Stranglers	Heroin
'God Smack'	Alice in Chains	Heroin
'Golden Brown'	The Stranglers	Heroin
'Mr Brownstone'	Guns 'N' Roses	Heroin
'The Needle And The Damage Done'	Neil Young	Heroin
'Waiting For The Man'	Velvet Underground	Heroin
'White Rabbit'	Jefferson Airplane	LSD, Magic Mushrooms
'I Love You Mary Jane'	Sonic Youth	Marijuana
'Mother's Little Helper'	The Rolling Stones	Prescription drugs
'Somebody Put Something In My Drink'	The Ramones	Unspecified
'Feel Good Hit Of The Summer'	Queens Of The Stone Age	Nicotine, Valium, Vicodin, Marijuana, Ecstasy & Alcohol

— TEN SCANDINAVIAN EUROPOP CLASSICS —

Abba – 'Waterloo'
The Herreys – 'Diggy-Loo Diggy-Ley'
Aqua – 'Barbie Girl'
Whigfield – 'Saturday Night'
A-ha – 'Take On Me'
Ace Of Base – 'All That She Wants'
Roxette – 'Listen To Your Heart'
Cardigans – 'Lovefool'
Europe – 'The Final Countdown'
Wannadies – 'You And Me Song'

— KIT SMASHERS —

Destroying your equipment onstage is as rock 'n' roll as resenting your parents, chasing groupies and choking on your own vomit. Here are the founders, the favourites and the current title-holders.

The Who
The Who were the first band to popularise smashing the hell out of your instruments as a means of expression. Drummer Keith Moon started to throw his drums around during his audition for the band and they never looked back. At the end of live shows, Moon's drum kit would be scattered across the stage while Pete Townshend would batter his guitar to smithereens and Roger Daltrey would swing his microphone around his head. Townshend claims this gimmick began accidentally when he broke his guitar on the low ceiling of a venue and had to make it look as if he'd done it on purpose.

Jimi Hendrix
After playing the guitar with his teeth or between his legs, Jimi would usually smash it into teeny tiny bits, and famously set his axe on fire onstage at the Monterey International Pop Festival in 1967.

Joe Perry (Aerosmith)
The Aerosmith axeman plays through the pain barrier to look the part on stage. He compares trying to break a Fender Stratocaster to smashing a baseball bat against a brick wall but claims that 'you're so loaded with adrenaline, you just keep doing it even though it hurts'.

Kurt Cobain (Nirvana)
Kit wrecking had a renaissance in the '90s with the emergence of grunge bands like Sonic Youth, Pearl Jam and, most famously, Nirvana. Frontman Kurt Cobain regularly took his frustration out on his guitar, as immortalised in the video for 'Lithium'.

And You Will Know Us By The Trail Of Dead
From Austin, Texas, this lot are the current holders of the kit-wrecking crown and have managed to progress the art form. Not only do they often break their guitars and scatter equipment onstage, but they have also been known to smash up entire venues during their shows. RAWK!

— KILLED BY ROCK?—
A BRIEF HISTORY OF BIZARRE ROCK DEATHS

Brian Jones: On the night of 2 July 1969, Rolling Stone Brian Jones was found dead in his swimming pool. He was 27. The coroner recorded a verdict of death by misadventure: drug and alcohol abuse had led to his drowning. Many of Jones's friends and relatives, plus thousands of his fans, have been disputing that verdict now for 35 years.

Anna Wohlin, Jones's girlfriend at the time, has always insisted that he was not drunk and hadn't taken any drugs. In her book, *The Murder Of Brian Jones*, she claims that Frank Thorogood, Jones's minder, murdered him by holding his head under the water – although she doesn't claim to have witnessed it. It is rumoured that Thorogood confessed to the murder on his deathbed in 1993, but no evidence of this confession has ever been produced. Author A E Hotchner, while researching a book on the Stones, tracked down a witness who claimed to have seen Jones killed by some of the builders who were working on his house – but this witness insists on remaining anonymous and has not spoken to the police. And, inevitably, there are those who believe it was suicide. Read all the theories at *www.brianjonesfanclub.com*.

Aaliyah: On 25 August 2001, 22-year-old R'n'B star Aaliyah was flying back from the Bahamas to Miami. Her pilot, convicted for crack cocaine possession just two weeks earlier, was not licensed to fly the Cessna, which, against the warnings of a baggage handler, had been overloaded. Aaliyah's huge bodyguard and his equally huge colleague, unable to squeeze their bulks up the aisle, sat down at the rear of the plane. With the weight of the luggage and bodyguards concentrated at one end and virtually no weight at the other, the plane dropped out of the sky almost as soon as it took off.

Terry Kath: On 23 January 1978, there was a party at the home of Terry Kath, Chicago's lead guitarist. At one point in the evening, he took out one of his guns to clean it. One of his guests nervously asked him to put it away. He reassured everyone that there was nothing to worry about as it wasn't loaded, and, to underline his point, he put the gun to his head and pulled the trigger. The gun *was* in fact loaded, and Kath was killed instantly. He was 31.

Mia Zapata: In July of 1993, the grunge band The Gits returned to Seattle after a very successful tour of the US West Coast. On the night of 6 July, Mia Zapata, their 27-year-old lead singer, was raped, strangled to death, and abandoned in the middle of a deserted street, her arms outstretched and ankles crossed in a crucifix pose. Her murder went on to become one of Seattle's most notorious, remaining unsolved for nearly ten years. The police finally caught up with the killer, Jesus Mezquia, in January of 2003. He was convicted on DNA evidence. The only motive appeared to be opportunity.

Michael Hutchence: At around noon on 22 November 1997, a maid at the Ritz in Sydney knocked on a guest's door. There was no answer, so she entered. The room was littered with bottles of drink and prescription drugs, and Michael Hutchence was hanging from the back of the door by his leather belt, naked and dead. He was 37. The coroner recorded a verdict of suicide, specifically ruling out the possibility of erotic auto-asphyxiation. However, the lack of a suicide note led to speculation – fuelled by Paula Yates, who refused to accept that her lover had committed suicide and fought in vain to have the verdict overturned. Paula herself died on 17 September 2000. The coroner recorded that she died of an accidental drug overdose, though, in a final irony, her post-mortem was inconclusive. She was 40.

— ONE HIT WONDERS —

Sometimes artists appear from nowhere, hit the top of the charts and promptly disappear again. Here are ten unforgettable songs from artists whose other work was rather less memorable:

'96 Tears' – ? And The Mysterians (1966)
'Black Betty' – Ram Jam (1997)
'Don't Fear The Reaper' – Blue Oyster Cult (1976)
'Groove Is In The Heart' – Deee-Lite (1990)
'Mickey' – Toni Basil (1982)
'Spirit In The Sky' – Norman Greenbaum (1969)
'This Wheel's On Fire' –Julie Driscoll, Brian Auger And The Trinity (1968)
'Turning Japanese' – The Vapors (1980)
'Voodoo Ray' – A Guy Called Gerald (1988)
'Your Woman' –White Town (1997)

— TALKING FOREIGN —

Sometimes when your dad moans 'I can't make out what they're singing about', he's got a point. The following huge hits were sung in foreign languages – except one, which was utter gibberish.

Year	Track	Artist	Language
1959	'La Bamba'	Richie Valens	Spanish
1969	'Je T'Aime... Moi Non Plus'	Serge Gainsbourg & Jane Birkin	French
1975	'Paloma Blanca'	George Baker selection/ Jonathan King	Spanish/English
1977	'Ca Plane Pour Moi'	Plastic Bertrand	French
1988	'Joe Le Taxi'	Vanessa Paradis	French
1996	'The Macarena'	Los Del Rio (1996)	Spanish
1998	'Sadness Part 1'	Enigma	Gregorian chants
2002	The Ketchup Song	Las Ketchup (2002)	Gibberish

— PATSY KENSIT'S HUSBANDS —

Actress Patsy Kensit, former singer of forgettable pop band Eighth Wonder, is more famous for her choice of partners than for any musical or actorly achievements. The 35-year-old actress has, so far, married:

Dan Donovan (Big Audio Dynamite): **1988–1991**
Jim Kerr (Simple Minds): **1992–1996**
Liam Gallagher (Oasis): **1997–2000**

— THE WORST DUETS OF ALL TIME... —

... according to *Q* Magazine

1. Cilla Black and Marc Bolan – 'Life's A Gas'
2. Motorhead and The Nolans – 'Don't Do That'
3. David Bowie and Bing Crosby – 'Peace On Earth'/'Little Drummer Boy'
4. Freddie Mercury and Montserrat Caballe – 'Barcelona'
5. Paul McCartney and the Frog Chorus – 'We All Stand Together'
6. David Bowie and Mick Jagger – 'Dancing In The Street'
7. Julio Iglesias and Stevie Wonder – 'My Love'
8. Mr Bean and Bruce Dickinson – 'I Want To Be Elected'
9. Elton John and RuPaul – 'Don't Go Breaking My Heart'
10. Elton John and Eminem – 'Stan'

— CAREFUL WITH THAT AXE, EUGENE —

Matt Bellamy, Muse
In early 2004, the diminutive frontman smacked himself in the teeth with his guitar. 'Mmph mmph mmph mmph,' he explained afterwards.

Robbie Williams
In 2001, Robbie was playing in Stuttgart when a fan managed to get past security and throw Williams into the photo pit. The deranged fan claimed that Williams was an imposter; the singer escaped with bruising.

James Hetfield
The Metallica frontman was badly burned at a 1992 gig in Montreal when an on-stage pyrotechnic went off at the wrong angle, enveloping the guitarist in flames.

Beck
In 2001, Beck finished his Wembley set in mid-air as his bassist held the singer high over his head. Unfortunately Beck came down on the bass guitar, causing internal bruising.

Frank Zappa
At a 1971 gig at London's Rainbow venue, Zappa was pushed from the stage by a fan. His larynx was crushed and his spine damaged, keeping him in a wheelchair for almost a year.

Alice Cooper
When a giant stage prop (a toybox) fell over during a 1975 Canadian gig, Cooper was knocked off the stage. He broke several ribs and needed stitches in his head.

Pete Townshend
During a late '80s gig in Washington, Townshend impaled his hand on his guitar's tremolo arm. Amazingly, he managed to avoid serious damage and escaped with a few stitches.

Bono
The U2 frontman dislocated his shoulder after slipping on a wet stage at a 1987 show in Washington, although the injury wasn't diagnosed until a week later. It wasn't the first injury on that tour: during rehearsals, Bono fell off the stage and hit his head on a spotlight, requiring stitches in his chin.

— DANCE CRAZES —

Dance	Origin
The Twist	'The Twist', Chubby Checker
The Hucklebuck	'The Hucklebuck', Herman Lubinsky
The Mashed Potato	'Mashed Potato Time', Dee Dee Sharp
The Cavern Stomp	Unique to the Cavern Club, Liverpool
The Funky Chicken	'Do The Funky Chicken', Rufus Thomas
The Slosh	'The Slosh', Bernadette
The YMCA	'YMCA', The Village People
Headbanging	Heavy metal, origin unknown
Air Guitar	Heavy metal, origin unknown
Stage diving	Origin unknown, but often credited to Iggy Pop
The Pogo	Punk
The Dying Fly	A favourite at early '80s school discos, invented by the TV show *Tiswas*
The Birdie Dance	'The Birdie Song', The Tweets
The Timewarp	*The Rocky Horror Picture Show*
Moonwalking	Michael Jackson*
The Agadoo	'Agadoo,' Black Lace
The Lambada	'Lambada', Kaoma
The Achy Breaky	'Achy Breaky Heart', Billy Ray Cyrus
Moshing	'Mash Down Babylon,' Bad Brains
Voguing	Madonna (who took the dance from New York clubs
The Macarena	'Macarena', Los Del Rios
The Riverdance	Michael Bloody Flatley
Ketchup Dance	'The Ketchup Song', Las Ketchup

* He may have popularised it, but he didn't invent it: the moonwalk was 'borrowed' from Jeffrey Daniels of Shalamar, who in turn borrowed heavily from James Brown

— ODD INSTRUMENTS —

Since the dawn of music people have been improvising with ways to make sound. And when rock was born things were no different. Skiffle is perhaps the best example, utilising as it did the washboard, the tea-chest/broom-handle, and perhaps most bizarre, the banjo.

Later in the '60s the Bonzo Dog Doo-Dah Band's hit 'Urban Spaceman' featured a length of hose whirred around the head of Viv Stanshall.

Hi-(ish) tech finally came to the charts with the Stylophone – but its most successful proponent wasn't Rolf Harris (whose 'wobble-board' would eventually surface on his string of hits in the '90s). No, the mini-keyboard from Dubreq provides the solo on David Bowie's first number one 'Space Oddity'. Equally unusual was the appearance of a pocket calculator on Kraftwerk's hit of the same name, and Switzerland's Trio's ultra-basic 'Da Da Da', like their German partners in electronic music, was entirely powered by Casio again, on this occasion via a pocket-sized-keyboard known as the VL-Tone.

The kazoo is an occasional guest on pop records but never more so than on the EP produced by the Temple City Kazoo Orchestra – a multi-member collective specialising in Kazoo-driven cover versions, including the Bee Gees' 'Staying Alive', Led Zep's 'Whole Lotta Love' and (of course) '2001 Sprach Kazoostra'.

'Ethnic' instruments, though widely used abroad – obviously – seldom appear in the UK. Even Nora Jones's dad Ravi Shankar failed to have a hit record in the UK. His instrument of choice – sitar – did at least appear on 'Norwegian Wood' as well as forming the basis for Monsoon's 1982 hit 'Ever So Lonely'.

And last, but certainly not least, the bagpipes reared their scary heads on the Royal Scots Dragoon Guards' version of 'Amazing Grace' as well on Paul McCartney's 'Mull Of Kintyre'.

— HIGHEST PAID DJS —

A job spinning records isn't enough for some people – take Alan Freed, for example, the man who reputedly coined the term rock 'n' roll. Embroiled in a payola scandal (taking money for paying records) he may not have been highly paid as a DJ, but did have a reputed $29,000 per day deal with Paramount Studios to make the film *Don't Knock The Rock* with Bill Haley and Little Richard.

Chris Evans was the highest-paid radio DJ, raking in £7,000 a day from the BBC, until he left following various very public disputes. That leaves Paul Oakenfold as the BBC's richest DJ, reportedly making £4.5 million per year, though much of this is down to extra-curricular activities like his *Perfecto* record label and DJ sets. Like his contemporaries Fatboy Slim, DJ Sasha, David Morales and Frankie Knuckles, he can expect to make as much as £20,000 for a single gig. Some big name DJs are rumoured to have been paid as much as £30,000 for a two hour set on Millennium Eve.

— THE BEST LIVE ALBUMS IN THE WORLD... EVER! —

As voted by readers of *Classic Rock* magazine:

1. *Live And Dangerous* – Thin Lizzy
2. *Strangers In The Night* – UFO
3. *Made In Japan* – Deep Purple
4. *If You Want Blood* – AC/DC
5. *How The West Was Won* – Led Zeppelin
6. *Live At Leeds* – The Who
7. *Unleashed In The East* – Judas Priest
8. *Space Ritual* – Hawkwind
9. *Exit Stage Left* – Rush
10. *Irish Tour* – Rory Gallagher

— MUSICAL GENRES INVENTED BY JOURNALISTS —

C86
Madchester
NWONW (New Wave Of New Wave)
Riot Grrrl
Shoegazing
Grunge
Brit Pop
The New Acoustic Movement

— FAT CHART-TOPPERS —

Pop music's not all skinny little girls, you know. Renne and Renato were as different from Britney Spears as you can possibly imagine; they were fat, Belgian, and in 1982 they were sitting at the top of the charts with their hit 'Save Your Love'.

Black Box hired a skinny bird to mime the words to their 1989 smash 'Ride On Time', but the real singer was Loleatta Holloway, who wasn't small.

When Meat Loaf starts dancing, get out of the way. His epic single 'I Would Do Anything For Love (But I Won't Do That)' reached number 1 on 17 October 1993 and stayed there for seven weeks.

2003 *Pop Idol* winner Michelle McManus weighs in at 15 stone, but that didn't stop her single 'All This Time' reaching number one in January 2004.

Other chart-topping salad-dodgers include:

Benny Hill – 'Ernie (The Fastest Milkman In The West)' (1971)
Barry White – 'You're The First, The Last, My Everything' (1974)
Elvis Presley – 'The Wonder Of You' (1970)
Mr Blobby – 'Mr Blobby' (1993)

— CHEERS GUYS, I'M OFF —

Ten musicians who dumped – or were dumped by – their bands:

Bill Berry	REM
Billy Idol	Generation X
Fish	Marillion
George Michael	Wham!
Ian McCulloch	Echo And The Bunnymen
John Lennon*	The Beatles
Peter Gabriel	Genesis
Roger Waters	Pink Floyd
Sting	The Police
Topper Headon	The Clash

* *Although it was Paul McCartney who shocked fans by announcing that he had left The Beatles, Lennon had already left the band in the aftermath of the Abbey Road sessions.*

— OBLIQUE STRATEGIES —

Brian Eno is the strange man who twiddled knobs for Roxy Music, pioneer of ambient music and one of the world's biggest producers, best known for his work with U2. The 'Oblique Strategies' cards he and painter friend Peter Schmidt came up with have become the stuff of legends. These cards contained slogans, reminders and suggestions for alternate ways of doing things, and were designed to be used to solve dilemmas or problematic situations in the recording studio. The messages ranged rom the straightforward to the ludicrously obscure and could be used by drawing a single card from the pack or going through the deck until inspiration was found. Here are a selection of examples from the original set.

Abandon normal instruments • Accept advice • A line has two sides • Balance the consistency principle with the inconsistency principle • Be dirty • Cluster analysis • Courage! • Define an area as 'safe' and use it as an anchor • Distorting time • Do nothing for as long as possible • Do something boring • Do we need holes? • Faced with a choice, do both • Feedback recordings into an acoustic situation • Get your neck massaged • Give way to your worst impulses • Imagine the music as a moving chain or caterpillar • Is the tuning appropriate? • Left channel, right channel, centre channel • Look at a very small object – look at its centre • Make a blank valuable by putting it in an exquisite frame • Make an exhaustive list of everything you might do and do the last thing on the list • Make a sudden, destructive unpredictable action; incorporate • Put in earplugs • Short circuit (example – a man eating peas with the idea they will remove his virility shovels them straight into his lap) • Tape your mouth • The inconsistency principle • Use an unacceptable colour • Water • You can only make one dot at a time

Blank cards were also included, to be filled in along the way!

— THE LONGEST-AWAITED ALBUMS EVER —

These rock illuminati were obviously far too busy being important to get in the studio and record an album:

Television – 13 Years

Pioneering New York post-punk group Television are generally regarded as one of the most important rock bands of the '70s, and more than a few eyebrows were raised when they regrouped to record a brand new album in 1992 – 13 years after their previous recording, 1978's *Adventure*.

The Blue Nile – 8 Years

These Glaswegian blues-poppers are not noted for being the most prolific in terms of album releases. After their 1984 debut *Walking On Rooftops*, it took them five years to bring out second album *Hats* and a further seven to follow that up with 1996's *Peace At Last*. No surprise, then, that it wasn't until August 2004 that they released their fourth album *High*, making a grand total of four albums in 20 years.

Peter Gabriel – 8 Years

After rejuvinating his solo career with 1992's *Us* album, Gabriel didn't release any new material until the turn of the millennium, although live album *Secret World* was a hit in 1994. 2000's *Ovo* was a collection of songs written for a huge multimedia show at London's Millennium Dome.

The Stone Roses – 5 Years

The Roses' eponymous 1989 debut set them up as godfathers of the 'Madchester' indie scene and they're still worshipped as gods by fans. After signing what was at the time one of the most lucrative record deals ever with Geffen Records, it took the band five years to come up with the follow-up, 1994's *Second Coming*.

Massive Attack – 5 Years

After the dub-tinged dance sounds of their debut album *Blue Lines* defined a generation of dance music and more or less created the term 'trip-hop', the laid-back Bristolians waited three years to bring out *Protection*, a further four to release *Mezzanine* and five before *100th Window* hit the shelves in 2003. If they continue to work to their current pattern, expect the next album in 2009.

— THE SPORT/ROCK CROSSOVER —

Rockers and their sporting obsessions:

Bruce Dickinson: Fencing
Cliff Richard: Tennis
Manic Street Preachers: Cricket*
Alice Cooper: Golf
Half Man Half Biscuit: Football**
Lars Ulrich (Metallica): Tennis***
Shaquille O'Neal: Basketball
Davey Jones (The Monkees): Horse racing****
Rod Stewart: Football

*Glamorgan's Matthew Maynard crops up regularly in
their songs, while Nicky Wire played football for Wales
under-16s
** Specifically Tranmere Rovers – they once famously
turned down an appearance on The Tube because
Tranmere were playing at home that day
***His father was a pro and he wasn't bad himself
**** Was an apprentice jockey*

— SIBLING RIVALRY —

The Jesus And Mary Chain	Jim & William Reid
Oasis	Noel & Liam Gallagher
Spandau Ballet	Martin & Gary Kemp
Heart	Ann & Nancy Wilson
The Beach Boys	Carl, Dennis & Brian Wilson
Bros	Matt & Luke Goss
Mel & Kim	Mel & Kim Appleby
Wilson Phillips	Carnie & Wendy Wilson
Embrace	Danny & Richard McNamara
All Saints	Nicole & Natalie Appleton
B*Witched	Keavy & Edele Lynch
INXS	Andrew, Tim & John Farris
Hanson	Isaac, Taylor & Zac Hanson
Orbital	Paul & Phil Hartnoll
The Carpenters	Karen & Richard Carpenter
The Corrs	Jim, Sharon, Caroline & Andrea Corr
Crowded House	Neil & Tim Finn
Radiohead	Jonny & Colin Greenwood

— PUMP UP THE VOLUME —

Danger: Rock 'n' roll is bad for your health. Turning up to 11 and rocking hard until it can't be rocked any harder can be a physically punishing business, particularly for the ears. The list of stars who have gone deaf, partially deaf or contracted other hearing disorders is huge, not surprising given what they do for a living. Here are a few sufferers:

Phil Collins: After over two decades of drumming and singing, the former Genesis man announced his retirement from touring in 2003, due to a critical deterioration in his hearing. Though not totally deaf, Collins is no longer able to play live and has turned to writing movie soundtracks instead.

The Who: It's hardly surprising given The Who's penchant for playing incredibly loudly, that their axeman Pete Townshend suffers from terrible hearing problems. He is completely deaf in one ear and has tinnitus in the other, caused mainly by an explosion when Keith Moon blew up his drum kit during a gig in the 60s. The Who's late bass player John Entwistle also had seriously depleted hearing, having to rely heavily on lip-reading.

Ted Nugent: The Amboy Dukes guitarist says, 'My left ear is pretty much whacked but I can still hear pretty good in my right'. The reason for this, apparently, is that he wore an earplug in his right ear because it was the one closest to his amp. Couldn't he afford two?

Stewart Copeland (The Police): Copeland has suffered from depleted hearing for years, resulting from drumming with The Police, but it hasn't stopped him writing several solo albums and composing TV and movie scores, including *The Equalizer*.

Bilinda Butcher (My Bloody Valentine): Bilinda, MBV's bass player, burst an eardrum onstage, losing the hearing in that ear. She initially regained hearing before it disappeared again. 'We all wear earplugs now,' she says. Stable doors and horses anyone?

Tinnitus, a serious hearing disorder resulting in a constant ringing in the ears, has been the scourge of many a rock musician. High-profile victims include: Neil Young, Bono and The Edge (U2), Eric Clapton, Tom Petty, Sting and Bob Mould (Husker Du and Sugar).

— TEN SONGS ABOUT CARS —

'Car Song' – Elastica
'Cars' – Gary Numan
'Drive' – The Cars
'Driving In My Car' – Madness
'Fast Car' – Tracy Chapman
'Jesus Built My Hotrod' – Ministry
'Killer Cars' – Radiohead
'Little Deuce Coupe' – The Beach Boys
'Little Red Corvette' – Prince
'Pink Cadillac' – Bruce Springsteen

— DRINK AND DRUGS —

Drink, drugs and rock 'n' roll proved a fatal mixture for these musicians:

Brian Epstein	Accidental overdose of brandy and pills, 1967
Jimi Hendrix	Choked on his own vomit after taking barbiturates, 1970
Janis Joplin	Heroin overdose, 1970
Gram Parsons	Heart failure due to tequila and morphine, 1973
Nick Drake	Suicide via overdose of antidepressants, 1974
Tim Buckley	Heroin overdose, 1975
Elvis Presley	Heart failure due to drugs overdose, 1977
Keith Moon	Accidental overdose of alcohol and barbiturates, 1978
Sid Vicious	Heroin overdose, 1979
John Bonham	Choked on own vomit after massive alcohol intake, 1980
Bon Scott	Choked on own vomit while drunk, 1980
Tim Hardin	Heroin overdose, 1980
Dennis Wilson	Drowned while drunk, 1983
Phil Lynott	Heart failure due to ongoing drug use, 1986
Steve Clark (Def Leppard)	Died in 1991 after years of alcoholism
Johnny Thunders	Drug overdose, 1991
Kirsten Pfaff (Hole)	Drug overdose, 1994
Jonathan Melvoin (Smashing Pumpkins)	Drug overdose, 1996
Rob Pilatus (Milli Vanilli)	Drug and alcohol overdose, 1998
Dee Dee Ramone	Accidental heroin overdose, 2002
John Entwistle (The Who)	Heart attack caused by cocaine, 2002

— STRAIGHT OUTTA ROYSTON —

Rockers can breed in the most unlikely places:
XTC – Swindon
Clinic – Crosby
Discharge – Stoke-On-Trent
Chicory Tip – Maidstone
Roman Holiday – Harlow
The Zombies – Royston
Lilac Time – Great Malvern
Tyrell Corporation – Redcar
Shiva – Huddersfield
Supermodel – Egham

— FAKE ACCENTS —

Change your accent and the public will ridicule you: it's a Law of Rock, as these musicians found out:

With Blur's *Parklife* album, Damon Albarn invited derision for his faux cockneyisms. The Streets' Mike Skinner, on the other hand, might actually be a Cockney, or at least a Londoner, but faces regular criticism for his accent anyway.

Lulu develops a rather sudden Scots brogue every time she sets foot north of the border. If it's an attempt to ingratiate herself, it fails dismally: the Scots are united by their hatred of both her accents.

Madonna's accent seems to have changed a little since she moved to England. The satirical US Press News (*www.uspressnews.com*) says: 'For the last six or seven years, Madonna has been speaking with a pseudo-English, rich snob, 1930s film star voice. It's very off-putting and sounds condescending to the listener.'.

Rosemary Clooney achieved fame through a frankly ridiculous fake accent, but very much against her wishes. Mitch Miller, Columbia's head of A&R in 1951, told Clooney she'd be recording 'Come On-A My House', a quasi-Armenian folk song. The song demanded an Armenian accent, which Clooney refused to do. According to her 1977 autobiography, when she told Miller she wouldn't do it, he responded by saying, 'Well, let me put it this way. I will fire you unless you show up tomorrow'. Within weeks, Clooney was riding high on one of the biggest-selling songs in America. It went on to sell more than a million copies.

— THE BEATLES VS THE STONES —

THE BEATLES

Song	Reached No. 1 on	Stayed there for
'From Me To You'	30/4/63	7 weeks
'She Loves You'	10/9/63	4 weeks
	26/11/63	2 weeks
'I Want To Hold Your Hand'	10/12/63	5 weeks
'Can't Buy Me Love'	31/3/64	3 weeks
'A Hard Day's Night'	21/7/64	3 weeks
'I Feel Fine'	8/12/64	5 weeks
'Ticket To Ride'	20/4/65	3 weeks
'Help!'	3/8/65	3 weeks
'Day Tripper'	14/12/65	5 weeks
'Paperback Writer'	21/6/66	2 weeks
'Eleanor Rigby'	16/8/66	4 weeks
'All You Need Is Love'	18/7/67	3 weeks
'Hello Goodbye'	5/12/67	7 weeks
'Lady Madonna'	26/3/68	2 weeks
'Hey Jude'	10/9/68	2 weeks
'Get Back' (with Billy Preston)	22/4/69	6 weeks
'The Ballad Of John And Yoko'	10/6/69	3 weeks

THE ROLLING STONES

Song	Reached No. 1 on	Stayed there for
'It's All Over Now'	14/7/64	1 week
'Little Red Rooster'	1/12/64	1 week
'The Last Time'	16/3/65	3 weeks
'(I Can't Get No) Satisfaction'	7/9/65	2 weeks
'Get Off Of My Cloud'	2/11/65	3 weeks
'Paint It Black'	24/5/66	1 week
'Jumping Jack Flash'	18/6/68	2 weeks
'Honky Tonk Women'	22/7/69	5 weeks

— LOOK OUT, ROGER! —

Roger Daltrey had a reputation for swinging his microphone around his head by the flex during instrumental sections of their live act. Ironically, while his colleagues Entwistle and Townshend managed to avoid being smacked in the chops by a Shure SM58, the singer suffered a fractured eye socket when Gary Glitter swung his microphone on stage and accidentally connected with Daltrey.

— TURN ON, TUNE IN, DROP OUT
THE MOST PSYCHEDELIC ROCKER EVER —

Syd Barrett: Founder and original driving force behind Pink Floyd, Barrett was responsible for psychedelic classics like *The Piper At The Gates Of Dawn*. After becoming far too drug-addled to perform he was invalided out of the band.

Julian Cope: Possibly rock's best example of an acid casualty. In his days with Scouse poppers The Teardrop Explodes in the late '70s and early '80s, his hallucinogen-guzzling habits were legendary. Julian became famous for onstage self-mutilation, crawling on beaches wearing nothing but a turtle shell and dressing up as a dog to 'bad vibe' then Prime Minister Margaret Thatcher out of office. Just say no, kids.

Jim Morrison: Morrison's lust for alcohol and LSD was a vital factor in his input to The Doors and to his eventual demise. While his contemporaries were using psychedelic drugs as a force for peace and love, Morrison saw them as a way of contacting the deepest recesses of his mind. His extreme indulgences and ego problems made his behaviour ever more erratic until he eventually withdrew to Paris, where he died at the age of 27.

Will Sinn: Perhaps not the best known on the list but for sheer psychedelic indulgence, he takes some beating. One half of Scottish duo The Shamen, his fondness for magic mushrooms was evident in the dubby sound and shamanic ethos of the band. His death, though, untimely, was perhaps fitting – he drowned swimming while extremely tripped out. Without his influence, The Shamen went on to become chart-topping pop monsters.

Brian Jones: The Rolling Stones' multi-instrumentalist began life as a high-octane rock 'n' roller, famous for fathering illegitimate children. As fame and suspected depression took their toll, Jones entered a downward spiral of drink and drugs and ended up in a confused haze, practically unable to pick up a guitar due to his mental and physical deterioration. A month after his official departure from the band, he was found dead in his swimming pool.

The Beatles: Their liking for getting high was behind their dramatic change from suited-and-booted popsters to the psychedelic sounds and beatnik philosophy of later work like *Sergeant Pepper*. The thinly veiled acid references of 'Lucy In The Sky With Diamonds' (LSD, geddit?), and falling in with the likes of spiritual guru the Maharishi and bizarre artist Yoko Ono were just some of the results of their intoxication.

— INDEX —